# Memory Power For Exams

*by*
William G. Browning, Ph.D.

INCORPORATED
LINCOLN, NEBRASKA    68501

ISBN    0-8220-2020-3
© Copyright 1983
by
**Cliffs Notes, Inc.**

# Preface

In school you are required to learn large amounts of information on many topics. But, as if that task were not enough, you also must quickly and accurately recall selected information for exams.

Exams are artificial, high-pressure situations. Few similar experiences exist outside the school setting. The memory systems described in this book will:

- Help you prepare for exams taken in school and elsewhere
- Enable you to quickly and accurately recall the information you need to do well
- Make studying easier and perhaps even more enjoyable for you

While a student, I used these memory systems with great success. As a study-skills counselor, I have taught these methods to thousands of students. I hope you will find them equally helpful.

*W. G. B.*

# Contents

## PART TWO: APPLYING THE METHODS

# Part One
# Learning the Methods

Part One is carefully constructed to take you step by step from basic concepts to an understanding of several useful memory strategies.

WORK THROUGH EACH STEP OF PART ONE.

To learn these memory strategies, you must actually work through each exercise in Part One in order before you go on to Part Two. Simply reading through the material is *not* enough. Only by exercising your mental muscles can you make these strategies your own.

As you study Part One, remember that you learn best when you divide your work into manageable chunks. It is natural to want to develop these memory skills quickly so that you can put them to use. However, because the concepts and exercises in Part One require a fair amount of mental energy, you should pace yourself to avoid "burnout."

Most of the exercises in Part One suggest a 15-minute delay before you take the memory test. To test your long-term memory, you may want to retake the test 24 or 48 hours later.

*Like our car, our memory is
something we take for granted
until it doesn't work.*

# INTRODUCTION

Mnemosyne was the Greek goddess of memory and the mother of the nine sister muses who presided over the arts and sciences. (Did she have trouble remembering all their names?) The words *mnemonic* (na-MON-ik) and *mnemonics* refer to any special methods used to assist the memory.

Memory systems are the electrical appliances of the study world. Just as dishwashers, vacuum cleaners, and other conveniences have eliminated much housework drudgery, so memory aids can relieve you of much homework drudgery.

## BENEFITS

The benefits of memory systems can be summed up by three F's: *Fast, Fun,* and *Fearless.*

**Fast.** In your studies you frequently encounter material that is slow and painstaking to learn. A lot of this information comprises details that you know you might be tested on: numbers, formulas, terminology, names of important people, places, and events, and so forth.

Most likely you've learned much of this information by rote, repeating it until it finally sinks in (you hope). *But by using memory aids you can avoid this time-consuming process of repeating information over and over again.*

**Fun.** When learning by frequent repetition, you are likely to become easily bored. You may even short-circuit the process and not study the material as well as you know you should.

One big advantage of mnemonic systems is that they can make memorizing more interesting. *Learning becomes fun because you are*

3

*using your imagination and creativity to help remember the information.* Each memory problem becomes an interesting puzzle for which you are seeking a solution. Any solution you develop is the right one, as long as it works for you.

**Fearless.** Perhaps most important, *memory aids increase your confidence that you are correctly remembering the information.*

Details often have no rhyme or reason. How do you remember, for example, that Rutherford discovered the nucleus and Chadwick the neutron and not the other way around? Mnemonic techniques help you make sense out of such facts and many other kinds of information too. Misremembering is far less likely because you have locked the information in securely.

## HOW MNEMONICS WORKS

Most memory aids are based on a simple fact: You remember something a lot better when you can make some sense out of it. For example, consider the following number.

$$729243812793$$

If you try to quickly memorize this number, you probably cannot do it very easily. But once you make some sense of the number, reconstructing it from memory is easy. Begin with the 3 on the right:

| $3 \times 243 =$ | $3 \times 81 =$ | $3 \times 27 =$ | $3 \times 9 =$ | $3 \times 3 =$ | |
|---|---|---|---|---|---|
| 729 | 243 | 81 | 27 | 9 | 3 |

As you become familiar with mnemonic systems you will see you can make sense out of almost every piece of information you want to remember. You simply select the correct memory tool to fit each case.

**An Example.** Below is an example of a mnemonic system in action. Use it to discover how effective mnemonic techniques are.

STEP ONE. Study the following list of 12 people paired with their occupations. For each name and occupation a symbol is provided, and a picture is described that somehow connects the two symbols for each pair. When memorizing the information, use these pictures or construct your own.

Try to visualize each picture as clearly as possible. For example, when you visualize the lump of coal, be specific. Visualize its color, size, and texture. And the flower—what color is it? What shape? Be sure to note what each symbol stands for. For instance, note that the piece of coal stands for the name *Coulter*.

STEP TWO. Very important! After visualizing all the pictures, go back and *review* them one more time, to firmly establish them in your memory. Also review the word that each symbol stands for.

STEP THREE. Wait at least 15 minutes. Then, without reviewing the material, take the test on page 89. (On the test, the people's names are listed in a different sequence and you are asked to give their occupations.)

### *Exercise 1-1*

*Use these pictures
or make your own*

| NAME AND CAREER | SYMBOL | COMBINED "PICTURE" |
| --- | --- | --- |
| 1. Coulter (KOL-ter) * | Coal | Flower growing out of a lump of coal |
| Botanist (studies plants) | Flower | |
| 2. King * | Crown | Person wearing crown helping someone across the street |
| Vice-President | Someone assisting | |
| 3. Godel * | God | God writing math formula on blackboard |
| Mathematician | Math formula | |
| 4. Barnes * | Barn | Teacher holding class in a barn |
| Educator | Teacher | |
| 5. Limon * | Lemon | Someone dancing around a lemon |
| Dancer | Someone dancing | |

6

| NAME AND CAREER | SYMBOL | COMBINED "PICTURE" |
|---|---|---|
| 6. Tarbell * | Tar-covered bell | Pen stuck through a black bell |
| Author | Pen | |
| 7. Cushing * | Cushion | A law book sitting on a cushion |
| Lawyer | Law book | |
| 8. Robeson * | Robe | An actor wearing a robe |
| Actor | Someone acting | |
| 9. Flagg * | Flag | Paintbrush wrapped in flag |
| Painter | Paintbrush | |
| 10. Brooke * | Brook (stream) | Soldier wading through a brook |
| General | Someone in military uniform | |
| 11. Woolton * | Sheep (wool) | Businessman riding on back of a sheep |
| Businessman | Someone in business suit | |
| 12. Nye * | Night | Someone laughing at night |
| Humorist | Someone laughing | |

**Outcome.** Obviously, you had one of two results on this exercise. Either the memory devices helped or they didn't.

If you scored six or more correct, the chances are that the mnemonic symbols helped your memory. If you scored below six or so on the exercise, maybe this kind of memory system does not work for you. But you won't know that until you have practiced the methods more. You may not have made vivid enough mental images. Later, you will have a chance to practice that skill. You won't know whether these methods work for you until you have used them.

## USES OF MNEMONICS

The exercise you have just completed shows one kind of information that mnemonics can help you remember—connecting people's names with other information you need to remember about the people.

Mnemonic systems can be used for a variety of other memory activities too—to help you remember vocabulary, terminology, historical events in proper sequence, formulas, numbers, spelling, grammatical rules, foreign language, and much more.

**Courses.** Memory aids will help you prepare for exams in your school courses. Once you have learned how to use these methods, you will find that you take exams with more ease and confidence.

**Standardized Tests.** Memory aids can help you prepare for and take standardized tests like the GED, ACT, and GMAT. As you review for one of these tests, you can easily memorize necessary formulas, concepts, and facts that are likely to be needed.

You will find it very helpful to use these mnemonic aids while studying the *Cliffs Test Preparation Guide* for the test you will be taking. Write your memory aids in the book next to the pieces of information they relate to.

**And Beyond.** Ideally, skills learned in school should be useful in your other activities. The techniques you will learn in this book will make you not only a more efficient student but a more effective individual too.

There are countless everyday situations in which you will find these memory techniques very helpful: for example, in remembering the names of people you are being introduced to, the steps for operating a machine, the way to someone's house, or the phone number of that special person you met at a party.

## HOW THIS BOOK IS ORGANIZED

This book is organized to make your learning of the techniques easy and efficient.

The first three chapters contain explanations, examples, and exercises for the various memory techniques available to you. *Read these chapters carefully. They will give you the necessary foundation of understanding.*

Each of Chapters 4 through 10 deals with a specific study area. For example, Chapter 4 covers "Remembering the Social Sciences" and Chapter 7, "Remembering Math." Select the chapters to study according to your particular needs at the moment. For example, if you are taking a chemistry class, read the "Chemistry" section of Chapter 4, "Remembering the Physical Sciences."

In Chapters 4 through 10, both examples and exercises are provided. The exercises give you a chance to develop mnemonic solutions to specific study-related problems. Sample solutions are *not* provided for all the items in these exercises because *any solution you develop which works for you is correct*. Take the practice tests for each exercise so you can find out how well your mnemonic devices are working.

If you are taking a class not covered in Chapters 4 through 10, look at Appendix 2 on page 113 to determine which section or sections are most similar to your subject. Of course, be sure to at least browse through other chapters as well. The more exposure you have to examples of the techniques, the faster you will develop an ability to apply the principles quickly and efficiently.

## BEING CREATIVE

I once attended a seminar at which the leader asked us to visualize ourselves each in some kind of container and describe it to the group. Without exception, we all described containers just large enough for us to fit into. Then the leader said, "My container is a thousand miles wide in all directions, filled with forests, meadows, and fields. The top is a hundred miles high, transparent so I can see the sky and stars!"

The point is, many of us, like the members of that seminar, tend to limit our imaginations. In using mnemonic devices, you must become used to doing just the opposite — expand your thinking and your creativity! Do not restrict your imagination within a small box. Let it travel miles in all directions, if necessary, to discover solutions to memory problems. Especially, don't be afraid of doing something "different."

## SOME IMPORTANT TERMS

Here are the definitions of some key terms used in this book.

**Association:** Connecting what you want to remember with something you already know. *Example:* Remembering the definition of *rehearse* (see below) because you know that the described behavior is what actors do when they rehearse.

**Group Portrait:** A technique of remembering a group of ideas, facts, names, etc., by constructing (mentally or on paper) a single image that combines symbols for all the individual items.

**Mnemonics:** (Na-MON-ics) Methods, other than by rote, used to help remember something.

**Mnemonigram:** (Na-MON-i-gram) Any drawing used to help remember a piece of information.

**Rehearse:** To review, usually from memory without benefit of notes, information you have studied. *Rehearsal greatly increases the probability that you will remember something.*

**Rote:** Memorizing by frequent repetition (possibly from the Latin word *rota,* meaning "wheel"). Contrasted with the mnemonic methods taught in this book, where repetition is only one part of the process.

**Solution:** Each mnemonic activity is like a puzzle for which a number of solutions are possible. A solution is a method used to help remember a piece of information. No two people are likely to come up with the same solution.

**Symbol:** A concrete representation of something intangible, so that it can be more easily visualized and remembered. *Example:* Intangible—happiness; symbol—someone smiling.

# WHAT YOU SHOULD KNOW ABOUT REMEMBERING

## KEY POINTS

**It Is Easier to Forget Than to Remember.** Perhaps you have been surprised by how little of a textbook chapter you remember when you have finished reading it. You'll be relieved to learn that your memory is not necessarily worse than normal. On the average, students remember only about half of the main points they read when they have just completed a typical textbook chapter. Then, of course, unless they review the material, their memory of that half becomes less clear with time.

One reason that students remember so little is that they often read through a textbook chapter without periodically stopping to process the information. (*Process* means doing something — anything — to help integrate the information into the memory.) If you do nothing within the first 20 seconds to help retain a new piece of information, you will usually forget it (for example, 20 seconds after someone tells you a phone number to dial, you probably cannot repeat the number unless you've tried in some way to remember it).

You may say, "But I *do* remember some things I read or hear without 'doing' anything with them!" Most likely, in these cases, either the new information has a special significance for you or you unconsciously associate it with something you already know about the subject. An example of something having special significance: A high school instructor told my class years ago a trick for remembering how to spell *necessary*. I still remember that particular event, probably because I had always had trouble spelling that word.

An example of an unconscious association: In a world history text you read, "War was the focus of life for Spartans. They practiced extreme self-denial to become more effective soldiers." If you already know that the word *Spartan* means "self-denying," you might remember the new information by automatically associating it with what you already know.

**The Sooner the Better.** Most forgetting occurs right away. Then, whatever you still remember tends to be lost more gradually. The sooner you process the new information in some way, the more you will retain for the long term. For instance, simply mentally reviewing key points from memory right after reading them greatly increases your long-term memory of them.

**The More the Better.** *Multiple coding* means that if you fix something in your memory in more than one way, you are more likely to remember it. People shown how to use multiple coding have been able to remember hundreds of pieces of new information. Take the case of the Spartans, mentioned earlier. One suggested way of "coding" is to relate the new information to a definition of the word. If you also remember a movie you've seen in which Spartans are shown to be militaristic, that is a second coding.

In most cases, a single coding with enough repetitions is sufficient. But for especially important information you may want to use a multiple-coding approach.

## A FORMULA FOR REMEMBERING

Follow the three steps below, and you are guaranteed—as much as possible—to remember the information.

- Decide what to remember.
- Select your memory strategy or strategies.
- Rehearse periodically.

**Decide What to Remember.** This step may sound easy, but in the school setting it has pitfalls at both extremes.

At one extreme are the students who highlight virtually every sentence on the textbook page. The page becomes so bright with streaks of yellow or pink that you practically need dark glasses to read it. These students are saying, in effect, that *everything* is important (or that they cannot tell the difference).

Like the person trying to buy too much with a limited paycheck, these students are spreading their mental energies too thin. Trying to remember every detail in every class can lead to frustration and failure (unless you have set all your spare time aside for studying and enjoy doing nothing else).

At the other extreme are the students who barely make two small marks on an entire page. Perhaps these students have decided to take the easy way out by assuming that little is worth noting. The trouble is that the instructor may have a very different point of view, and she or he is the one who prepares the tests.

Somewhere in between is that magical zone where the proper amount of attention to detail will reap large rewards on tests. But how do you decide what is the "proper" amount?

First, analyze the course. Determine as best you can what kinds of information will be included on the tests. Here are some questions you should seek answers to.

- What proportion of the test items will come from the lectures and what proportion from the readings?
- What kinds of information will be stressed on the test?
- How detailed will some of the test items be? (For example, will they include numbers, names of people, relatively unimportant terminology?)
- Will the test include items on only the material covered since the previous test, or will it deal with all the subject matter covered so far in the course?

You have several ways to find answers to these kinds of questions.

- Watch for clues from the instructor. Whatever he or she emphasizes, underlines on the board, repeats, and so forth, is likely material for a test.
- Be an alert listener and reader. Often an instructor will tell the class important information about the tests or will write it in a handout. Watch for these sources of information.

- Ask the instructor! Yes, general questions about the scope of the test certainly are permissible. Begin, perhaps, by saying that you need such-and-such information in order to study more effectively. (That's true.)
- Ask students who have already taken the class from the same instructor. Be sure to ask specific questions and steer the students away from useless generalities. Select bright, successful students to question.
- When you take a test in the course, note the kinds of questions being asked. As soon as possible after the test, write some notes in which you try to answer questions like those beginning on page 12.

These suggestions are only examples. You certainly can add other strategies of your own. The point is that before you can decide what to remember, you should have some idea of which pieces of information are likely candidates for test items.

**Select Your Memory Strategy or Strategies.** Once you have chosen a piece of information for memorizing, your next step is to select a memory strategy or strategies. Chapters 3 through 10 cover this process in detail.

**Rehearse Periodically.** *Rehearse* means repeat the information, preferably from memory. Rehearse the new information when you first encounter it and then at regular intervals to keep the information sharp in your memory. *No formula for remembering should be without this step.* REHEARSAL IS THE SINGLE MOST EFFECTIVE WAY TO LOCK NEW INFORMATION INTO YOUR MEMORY.

**Summary.** The formula for remembering is *decide, select,* and *rehearse.* Suppose you read in your geology text, "The Paleozoic (Pay-lee-uh-ZO-ik) era was characterized by invertebrates, animals having no backbones."

First, you *decide.* "Based on what the instructor has emphasized in the lectures, this might be on the test. I'll learn it." (You might highlight the information in your book to indicate your decision.)

Next, you *select.* "*Paleozoic* sounds like 'pay Lee.' I'll imagine someone paying Lee with a bunch of invertebrates."

Finally, you *rehearse*. After reading the rest of the text page, you rehearse by thinking, "Pay Lee with invertebrates. Paleozoic period had invertebrates." You visualize the scene in your mind's eye, thus securing the association in your memory. Over the next few days, you rehearse the association several more times to make sure it is secure.

# THE MEMORY METHODS

*Rave:* "To speak with wild enthusiasm." After mastering the techniques in this book, you will be able to "speak with wild enthusiasm" about your memory.

Virtually all the mnemonic methods discussed in this book are derived from one or a combination of the techniques in the R.A.V.E. acronym. (An acronym is a word each letter of which stands for another word.) The letters in the acronym R.A.V.E. stand for:

- Rehearse: Repeat and Review
- Associate
- Visualize
- Encluster

## REHEARSE: REPEAT AND REVIEW

Rehearsal is mentioned first in the acronym, and appropriately so, because you need to rehearse, no matter what other memory methods you select. Without this key method all else is likely to fail.

Suppose you read in your psychology text, "W. H. Sheldon gave names to the three main human body types. Endomorphs are soft and round, mesomorphs are muscular and strong, and ectomorphs have long, fragile bodies." You associate the name *Sheldon* with *shell* and visualize three different shapes of shells. Then you think, "Endomorphs have soft 'ends,' mesomorphs, being muscular, can make a 'mess' of you, and ectomorphs are fragile, like an echo."

The first time you try to rehearse these associations from memory —even shortly after your first encounter—your thought process may go something like this.

Shell. I think it was Shelton or Sheldon. Three body types. Endo
—endo what? Endodorphs? Anyhow, they're soft. What were the
other two? Echo. Echodorphs? Thin? The third I don't remember.
Starts with an "M," I think.

Then when you check the text for the correct answers, you will pay
particular attention to the parts you got wrong or were not sure about.
"Sheldon! Not Shelton," and so forth.

That first rehearsal and checkup has a powerful effect. It will greatly
sharpen your memory of the information. Most likely, a second rehearsal
will have no errors or very few, which will be pounced on and corrected.
From then on, it's a matter of rehearsing periodically to keep the associations strong and to build your confidence that you do, indeed,
know the material.

## ASSOCIATE

Many memory experts believe that association is an essential step in
remembering something for a long time. *Associating* means connecting
new information or images with something you already know. We all
frequently make associations, often without realizing it.

An example illustrates this process. I had often read that if you make
a very bizarre, unusual mental image, you remember it better than you
would a more commonplace one. This information became my "known."
Then I read that according to research studies a more unusual image is *not*
remembered any better. Because I quickly associated this new information with what I already knew, the new information was securely locked
into my memory.

Experts have a relatively easy time remembering new information in
their field because they can usually find some related, known information
with which to associate the new information.

**Natural and Artificial Associations.** The case just mentioned about
the unusual images is an example of a *natural* association. A natural
association is one in which the connection does not have to be forced; it
occurs naturally. To make an *artificial* association you must use your
imagination and create an association where one did not exist before.

The following example illustrates the difference between natural and
artificial associations. You read in your geology text that *magma* is the

molten, liquid matter under the earth's crust. If you happened to know that the prefix *mag* means *to knead,* you could easily make a natural association to remember the definition of magma: Magma is molten; therefore it can be "kneaded."

But if you do not know the meaning of *mag,* you can make an artificial association. First, you must ask yourself what the prefix *mag* reminds you of: magnesium? magnet? "mag" automobile wheels? maggot? Maggie? The word you choose depends on your personal universe of experience and knowledge.

Let's assume that you choose the word *magnet.* Then, you might visualize a magnet floating on some molten, liquid matter. Later, when you think of the word *magma,* it will remind you of a magnet, which you will visualize connected to molten matter.

**Logical Associations.** Closely related to natural associations are logical associations, or the "that makes sense" associations. However, instead of making an association with a specific piece of information, you are associating the new information with a general feeling that it makes sense or fits in with your view of how things ought to be. Suppose you read in your psychology text that adolescents are more likely to feel unwanted by their parents if their parents are either extremely controlling or extremely ignoring. You might remember this fact by saying to yourself that it seems logical. It fits. It makes sense.

**Use of Symbols.** Symbols make abstract concepts, ideas, names and feelings more tangible and concrete. When you want to tell people you love them, you might send them a valentine heart. If you want to express patriotic feelings, you might display a flag.

Two propositions are central to the use of mnemonic systems.

- You can remember something better if you can make it concrete.
- Any idea, concept, name, fact, etc., that you want to remember can be made concrete through the use of a symbol.

In the example above of magma, we chose the magnet as a symbol to make a connection between the word and its definition. The name/occupation exercise on pages 5–6 uses symbols to help remember the names and occupations of the people. Anything, no matter how abstract, can be symbolized to make it concrete. Some things require more imagination and creativity than others, but the translation *can* be made.

**Methods.** One way to translate an abstraction into a symbol is by thinking of something concrete that could represent the abstraction. An image of a muscular person might be used to represent *strength*. An image of someone kneeling might be used to symbolize *humility*. Another method is to use a symbol that sounds exactly like or similar to the abstract word. This technique often is used with people's names and with vocabulary. For instance, the name *Smith* could be translated into an image of a blacksmith. Or the name *Farnesworth* could be translated into the similar sounding *farms-worth*.

It generally is more effective to make a symbol out of the first part of a name or word instead of the ending part, if you have a choice. With the name *Gilliland,* for example, it would be more effective to make a symbol out of *Gill* than out of *land*. Naturally, the most effective approach is to make a symbol, if possible, that combines all parts of the name. The name *Klingelhut,* for instance, could be translated into someone *clinging* to a *hut*.

Of course, any method that works is appropriate. For example, if the name *Smith* reminds you of a celebrity or someone else with the same name, that person could be used as your symbol.

### *Exercise 3-1*

Below is a list of 20 abstract names and concepts. Symbols are provided for the first ten as examples. Develop symbols for the other ten. Remember, whatever you choose is correct, as long as it works for *you* — as long as it helps *your* memory.

| ABSTRACT | SYMBOL |
|---|---|
| 1. Intelligence | Brain |
| 2. Sadness | Someone crying |
| 3. Peace | Dove |
| 4. Ignorance | Dunce cap |
| 5. Security | Padlock |
| 6. Robinson | Robin (bird) |
| 7. Eyberg | Eye on iceberg |
| 8. Fowler | Hunter (of fowl) |
| 9. Hastings | Someone in a hurry (hasty) |
| 10. Martin | Martian (from Mars) |

19

| ABSTRACT | SYMBOL |
|---|---|
| 11. Tired | |
| 12. Language | |
| 13. Happiness | |
| 14. Justice | |
| 15. Speed | |
| 16. Taylor | |
| 17. Howe | |
| 18. Franklin | |
| 19. Colewell | |
| 20. Bronson | |

## VISUALIZE

R.A.V.E.: Rehearse...Associate...and now, Visualize. Visualizing and associating are very closely connected in the memory process. The previous section discusses the use of symbols to make abstractions concrete. You make something concrete so you can visualize it in your mind's eye.

People remember things better when they can picture them in their minds. That is why in large parking lots the sections are sometimes identified by animal pictures. A person can remember an owl or elephant, which can be visualized, better than a more abstract number or letter. For some people, learning how to visualize clear, specific mental images takes some practice. Remember:

THE MORE VIVID THE MENTAL IMAGE,
THE MORE LIKELY YOU WILL BE ABLE TO RECALL IT.

### Exercise 3-2

Below is an exercise to practice making vivid mental images.

STEP ONE. Study the pairs below. Visualize each object in the left-hand column connected somehow with the object in the right-hand column (for example, for the first one a gun pointing at an orange or an orange stuck on the gun's barrel).

Notice that the objects in the right-hand column are very similar to each other; some have the same shape, others the same color. So you must visualize the objects very clearly and specifically if you are not going to confuse one for another. Visualize the texture of the orange, the slightly different shape of the lemon, and so forth.

1. Gun _____Orange
2. Shoe _____Lemon
3. Tree _____Yellow tennis ball
4. Door _____Baseball
5. Hive _____Apple
6. Sticks_____Yellow rubber ball with red stripe

STEP TWO. After studying these six pairs wait at least 15 minutes; then take the test on page 89. On the test, you are given the objects in the left-hand column (in a different order) and must fill in the correct right-hand objects.

For additional practice, construct other exercises similar to this one. For the right-hand column you could use faces of people or a series of similar objects.

**Using Mnemonigrams.** Mnemonigrams (na-MON-i-grams) help you to make the visualizing process more effective. A mnemonigram is a picture that depicts a mnemonic association. Once such a picture is drawn, many people find the association easier to remember. You do *not* have to be an artist (whatever that is) to draw mnemonigrams. Simple stick figures can be quite effective.

You read in your psychology text, "Charles Spearman believed that intelligence is a single trait he called 'g,' for general intelligence. He said that intelligence is psychical energy, possessed in differing amounts by different people. More difficult tasks require greater amounts of psychical energy." Your symbol for Spearman might be a man holding a spear. You could draw the following mnemonigram to associate Spearman, the "g" factor, and psychical energy (symbolized by the smoke coming out of the target).

One rehearsal of the meaning of this mnemonigram should lock it firmly in your memory.

*Exercise 3-3*

On a separate piece of paper, draw a mnemonigram to depict the following information.

Freud believed that the human mind has three parts which interact. He called them the id, the ego, and the superego. These parts don't really exist in the brain, but instead are used to try to explain behavior. The id is concerned with instinctual drives. Not knowing right from wrong, it operates on the pleasure principle. The ego tries to figure out how the selfish needs of the id can be fulfilled. The superego is the conscience, acting like a policeman to oppose the selfish desires of the id.

To test your recall, turn to page 89 at least 15 minutes after *rehearsing* the information from memory.

For other examples of mnemonigrams, see pages 24, 26, 34, and 77. Experience will show you whether mnemonigrams improve your recall of mnemonic images.

## ENCLUSTER

R.A.V.E.: Rehearsal is an essential step, no matter what memory methods you choose. Association and visualization are two parts of the mnemonic method you probably will use most often. Enclustering, the final technique in the R.A.V.E. acronym, is a specialized method you probably will seldom use. However, for some sets of information it can be very helpful.

*Enclustering* means organizing pieces of related information according to some sort of logical order. Pieces often are grouped into categories by similarities. Sometimes the organization forms a hierarchy from more general to more specific.

Usually in the form of a diagram, enclustering is more logical than visual. You are not translating abstractions into symbols, and you are not creating visual images. You will have to try the method to see whether it helps your recall.

Suppose, for example, you wanted to encluster the seven mental abilities postulated by L. L. Thurstone. The seven abilities are:

*Word fluency:* The ability to use words with ease in speaking and writing.
*Verbal meaning:* The ability to understand ideas conveyed with words.
*Numerical ability:* The ability to work with numbers and do simple arithmetic.
*Memory:* The ability to retain, recognize, and recall information.
*Reasoning:* The ability to use past experiences to solve complex problems.
*Space perception:* The ability to correctly perceive size and spatial relationships.
*Perceptual speed:* The ability to identify objects quickly.

After studying these seven traits, you might develop the following diagram.

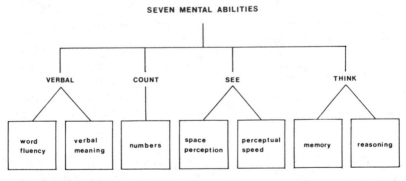

SEVEN MENTAL ABILITIES

VERBAL — COUNT — SEE — THINK

word fluency — verbal meaning — numbers — space perception — perceptual speed — memory — reasoning

When reconstructing this diagram from memory, you first need to remember only four categories instead of seven. Then, for each of these categories, you need to recall only one or two mental abilities. Using such a diagram reduces the number of information pieces you need to remember at each stage.

## APPLICATION

If you have carefully studied the information in the book to this point, you understand the basic concepts involved in using mnemonic systems. The next step is to learn how to apply these techniques to the various memory challenges you face in your school work. Most school-related memory challenges fall into one of the following categories.

- Remembering pairs, connecting —
  names with who the people are
  vocabulary and terminology with their definitions
  spelling with words
  numbers with what they stand for
- Remembering groups of information, such as —
  sequences of steps
  sequences of events
  clusters of facts, ideas, concepts, etc.
- Remembering groups and pairs combined
- Remembering rules, procedures, and principles

## REMEMBERING PAIRS

You almost never need to remember a single, isolated piece of information. With very few exceptions you really want to remember at least two things that are connected. For example, remembering the name *Picasso* does no good unless you can recall who he was. Remembering the word *loquacious* is useless unless you can connect it with its definition. Remembering the date 1066 is relevant only if you also remember that the Norman Conquest occurred that year.

Therefore, the first level of mnemonic systems deals with remembering pairs. Below are discussed the categories of pairs you need to remember most often in school.

**Connecting Names with Who the People Are.** You will recall from the earlier discussion (page 18) that when developing a mnemonic symbol for a name you normally use:

- A same-sounding or similar-sounding word, or
- An acquaintance, celebrity, etc., who has the same or a similar name and whose face you can easily visualize

Fortunately, many people's names are or have embedded in them words that can easily be turned into symbols: for example, Carpenter, Flaten, Fleetwood, Leek, and Marshall. Even with less obvious names you usually can think of a symbol that will remind you of the name.

Then, you need to think of a symbol to represent the information you want to remember about the person. You can connect the two symbols with a mental picture or by drawing a mnemonigram.

### Exercise 3-4

Below are listed the names of 15 individuals and a contribution each made to his or her field. Symbols and mnemonic picture descriptions are provided for the first five pairs, and a mnemonigram is given for the first one. Using separate paper if necessary, write symbols and picture descriptions or mnemonigrams for the other ten.

| NAME ⟶ | SYMBOL | CONTRIBUTION ⟶ | SYMBOL | MNEMONIC PICTURE |
|---|---|---|---|---|
| 1. Hersey | Hershey bar | Wrote *A Bell for Adano* | Bell | Hershey bar melting on bell |

*Mnemonigram*

| NAME ⟶ | SYMBOL | CONTRIBUTION ⟶ | SYMBOL | MNEMONIC PICTURE |
|---|---|---|---|---|
| 2. Hutton | Hut on | Studied earth movements | Earth moving | Hut on moving earth (earthquake) |
| 3. Longfellow | A tall fellow | Wrote *Paul Revere's Ride* | Paul Revere on horseback | Tall Paul Revere on horseback |
| 4. Hals | Halls | Painted the *Laughing Cavalier* | Laughing Cavalier | Laughing Cavalier in hall |
| 5. Copernicus | Copper nickels | Described sun-centered planetary system | Sun | Sun shining on copper nickel |

| NAME ——→SYMBOL | CONTRIBUTION ——→SYMBOL | MNEMONIC PICTURE |
|---|---|---|
| 6. Moliere | Wrote *The Miser* | |
| 7. Lear | Wrote *The Owl and the Pussy-Cat* | |
| 8. Curie | Discovered radium | |
| 9. Dalton | Conceived modern notion of atoms | |
| 10. Wren | Designed St. Paul's Cathedral — London | |
| 11. Mayer | Stated principle of conservation of energy | |
| 12. Rodin | Sculpted *The Thinker* | |
| 13. Botticelli | Painted *Birth of Venus* | |
| 14. Chekhov | Wrote *The Cherry Orchard* | |
| 15. Hertz | Demonstrated existence of radio waves | |

Check your recall of these names and contributions. After you have *rehearsed* the 15 pictures from memory, wait at least 15 minutes and then turn to page 89.

**Connecting Vocabulary and Terminology with Definitions.** The procedure for remembering vocabulary and terminology is very similar to that for remembering names. As is discussed on page 16, you should first look for a natural association; if you cannot think of any, then use an artificial association: Develop symbols for the word and its meaning and connect them in a mental or drawn picture. Then, rehearse the picture and its meaning until they are firmly locked in your memory.

Suppose that you want to remember that the word *scintillate* (SINT-uh-late) means to give off sparks. The word *scintillate* reminds you of *sent late*. As is usually the case with vocabulary, the symbol for the definition is obvious — sparks or something sparkling.

But how do you make the words *sent late* into a concrete image you can visualize? You might imagine someone running with a package that has the word *late* written on it and is giving off sparks. Following is a possible mnemonigram.

*Exercise 3-5*

Below are 12 terms and vocabulary words. Symbols and a picture description are provided for the first five. Using separate paper if necessary, write symbols and picture descriptions or mnemonigrams for the remaining seven.

| WORD | ⟶ SYMBOL | DEFINITION AND SYMBOL | PICTURE |
|------|----------|----------------------|---------|
| 1. Torpor (TOR-per) | Torn purr (cat) | Sluggishness, dullness | Cat made sluggish by being "torn" |

| WORD ⟶ SYMBOL | | DEFINITION AND SYMBOL | PICTURE |
|---|---|---|---|
| 2. Igneous | Ignited | Rock formed when molten material solidifies | Rock cooling but still ignited |
| 3. Palliate | Pal, he ate | To reduce the pain or intensity of | Pal reducing pain with food (he ate) |
| 4. Septum | Septic tank | Wall separating two cavities | Septic tank with walls |
| 5. Captious (KAP-shush) | cap, shush | tricky, deceiving | Burglar wearing cap, with finger to lips, saying "shush" |
| 6. Moraine | | Ridge of rocks and mud deposited by a glacier | |
| 7. Gibbous | | Phase of the moon more than half full | |
| 8. Mummery | | Ridiculous ceremonies | |
| 9. Hirsute (her-SOOT) | | Hairy, shaggy | |
| 10. Aorta | | Main artery leaving the heart | |
| 11. Probity (PRO-buh-tee) | | Reliability (of a person) | |
| 12. Fulsome | | Offensive (based on insincerity) | |

Check your recall of these words and their meanings. After you have *rehearsed* the 12 pictures from memory, wait at least 15 minutes and turn to page 89.

28

**Connecting Spellings and Words.** You can improve your spelling in many ways. For example, the more you write—and check unsure spellings—the less spelling is likely to be a problem. Also, spelling rules, available in most English handbooks, can eliminate many misspellings.

Mnemonic techniques are very effective in remembering how to spell your "demon" words, the ones that you continually seem to have trouble with.

To remember how to spell a word, look for an embedded word or part of a word. Suppose you frequently misspell *environment* as *enviroment*. Notice that the word *iron* is embedded in *environment*. Now make a sentence that connects the whole word and the embedded one: for instance, *"Iron ore makes the environment reddish."*

Of course, you do not have to limit your associations to embedded *words*. Any connection that helps you remember the spelling is appropriate. Consider, for instance, the word *parallel*. A common misspelling is *paralel*. You could use the embedded word *all* and say, *"All* railroad tracks are par*all*el." But another possible association is to say, "The two *l*'s next to each other in *parallel* are parallel."

Another useful method is to pronounce a word the way it is spelled. If, for example, you pronounce *environment* so that you hear the *ron,* you are less likely to omit the *n*. To remember that necessary has a *c* instead of an *s,* you might say to yourself, "NECK-a-sary."

## *Exercise 3-6*

Below are 12 commonly misspelled words. The usual trouble spots are underlined. The first five are completed as examples. Develop associations for the other seven.

| WORD | ASSOCIATION |
|------|-------------|
| 1. A<u>c</u>quire | <u>A</u>ctors <u>ac</u>quire speaking skills. |
| 2. Con<u>sc</u>ien<u>t</u>ious | A <u>sc</u>ien<u>t</u>ist must be con<u>sc</u>ien<u>t</u>ious. |
| 3. Gramma<u>r</u> | Don't <u>mar</u> your gram<u>mar</u>. (or) There is no gram<u>mar</u> on <u>Mar</u>s. |
| 4. Disapp<u>o</u>int | The <u>sap</u> <u>po</u>inted and was disapp<u>o</u>inted. |

| WORD | ASSOCIATION |
|---|---|

5. Fulfill      Fulfill can be full without the second
*l* in full

6. Accommodate
7. Suppress
8. Temperament
9. Personnel
10. Precede
11. Guidance
12. Medieval

Check your recall of these spellings. After you have *rehearsed* the 12 words from memory, wait at least 15 minutes and turn to page 89.

**Connecting Numbers with What They Stand For.** Numbers are a particularly challenging area in which to apply mnemonics. Unlike names, vocabulary, and spellings, numbers seldom have anything about them that can be easily used for an association. Consider 1898, the date of the Spanish-American War. For most students this number has nothing about it to help relate it to the event. This problem occurs with many numbers.

Very complex phonetic systems have been developed to help remember numbers. But these systems require a long time to learn and are useful only if someone must remember many numbers. Since history courses do not usually emphasize the recall of dates, such a system is seldom worth learning.

However, sometimes you do need to learn a number, and some simpler mnemonic devices are available.

**Number-Letter Key.** On the following page are listed letter equivalents for 1 through 9 and zero. The matchings are based on similar shapes between numbers and letters. For instance, a *1* resembles an *l*, a *2* on its side looks likes an *N*, a *3* on its side resemble an *M*, and so forth.

| Number | Letter |
|:------:|:------:|
| 1 | ⅄ |
| 2 | N |
| 3 | ⋔ |
| 4 | + |
| 5 | S |
| 6 | C |
| 7 | ⅂ |
| 8 | ß |
| 9 | ∪ |
| 0 | O |

Suppose you want to remember that the American Revolution ended when the British were defeated in 1781. With dates beyond 999 you can omit the beginning *1* since it is obvious. So you need to translate only *781* into letters:

Next, make a sentence or phrase in which the words begin with the letters indicated. Try to use words that connect the number with the thing or event it represents. For example:

<u>F</u>allen <u>B</u>ritish <u>l</u>eave

### Exercise 3-7

Although most students seldom have to learn dates in school, dates are a handy source for practicing numerical recall. Below are listed 12 dates and the events they represent. The first five have been completed, using the number-letter key. Find solutions for the other seven dates.

Remember that the initial *1* is dropped in each date beyond 999.

| DATE | EVENT | KEY LETTERS AND WORDS |
|---|---|---|
| 1. 1119 | Knights Templar founded to protect pilgrims on their travels | llg = Let learners go (*Think:* The Knights Templar let (allowed) the learners (pilgrims) go on their travels.) |
| 2. 1338 | Start of the Hundred Years' War | MMB = Many military battles |
| 3. 1543 | Copernicus claims the sun is the center of our system | STM = Sun the middle |
| 4. 1517 | Luther touches off the Reformation | SlF = Started Lutheran faith |
| 5. 1584 | Raleigh tries unsuccessfully to establish a colony in the New World | SBT = Settlers become troubled (*Think:* Raleigh's settlers became troubled and had to return to England.) |
| 6. 1215 | King John accepts the provisions of the Magna Carta | |
| 7. 410 | The Goths invade and pillage Rome | |
| 8. 1054 | A split occurs between the Eastern and Western churches | |
| 9. 1534 | Henry VIII establishes the Church of England | |
| 10. 1815 | Napoleon is defeated at Waterloo | |
| 11. 1789 | Beginning of the French Revolution | |
| 12. 1936 | Start of the Spanish Civil War | |

You can check your recall of these dates. After you have *rehearsed* the 12 dates from memory, wait at least 15 minutes and turn to page 91.

For other examples on numbers, see page 71.

**Decimals.** The number-letter key method can be used for remembering numbers that include a decimal. In these numbers, insert a word beginning with a *P* (for *point*) where the decimal is located. For example, suppose you want to remember that one foot equals 0.3048 meters, or "point 3048 meters." This number would translate into P M O T B. An example of a connecting sentence would be, "Put meter on the boot." The word *boot* associates *meter* with *foot*.

**Personal Associations.** Another technique for remembering numbers is based upon the fact that all of us have a collection of meaningful numbers in our memories. These can sometimes be used to make associations with new numbers. For example, the Mexican War took place in 1848. You might remember that date by associating the 48 with the number of contiguous (connecting) states in the United States.

When studying a number for recall, see whether all or part of it reminds you of a meaningful number already in your memory.

## REMEMBERING GROUPS

In your studies you often will want to do more than just connect a single pair of items. For example, in history you may want to remember, in correct sequence, a long series of events. In chemistry you may want to remember the steps required to achieve a certain chemical reaction. In literature you may want to remember the order of key events in a novel.

Several mnemonic techniques are available for working with groups of information. In fact, there are so many choices that you may feel overwhelmed at first. However, as you become more familiar with these methods, you will learn to select the ones that best fit your needs and personal learning style.

**Sequential Versus Nonsequential.** Groups of information that you have to remember fall into two main categories: sequential and nonsequential. Sequential information must be remembered in a particular order, or sequence: the colors of the light spectrum, for instance, or the succession of monarchs in a period of history.

On the other hand, nonsequential information can be learned and recalled in any order you wish. Suppose you wanted to learn the names of the animal classes in the Molusca phylum. Because these classes are not in any sequence, the order in which you recall them is unimportant.

Some mnemonic systems are mainly useful for recalling nonsequential information, while others can be used for both sequential and nonsequential.

**Overview.** The methods discussed for remembering groups of information are:

**Group Portrait:** This method is an extension of the images used to remember pairs. More symbols are added to the "picture." (Usually for nonsequential information.)

**Peg Words:** By using a prelearned sequence of symbols, you can connect, or "peg," a piece of information to each symbol. (For sequential or nonsequential information.)

**Linking Symbols:** You link a series of symbols, one pair at a time, to form a chain. (For sequential and nonsequential information.)

**Story:** You make a story in which key words relate to the main points you want to remember. (For sequential and nonsequential information.)

**Sentences with Key Letters:** The letter that begins each word is the same as the letter of an item you wish to remember. (For sequential and nonsequential information.)

**Acronym:** One or more words or nonsense syllables are developed in which each letter is the same as the first letter of an item to be remembered. (Usually for nonsequential information unless items to be learned in sequence happen to coincidentally form an acronym.)

**Using Group Portraits.** A group portrait is a mental picture or mnemonigram in which a number of symbols are combined. Experience will show you how many symbols you can handle in a single picture. If you are trying to remember more than four or five pieces of information, you probably should consider using a different mnemonic method. Also, group portraits do not work well for sequential information.

Suppose you want to be able to quickly recall four poems by Robert Frost. Each poem represents a theme you could write about on an essay exam. The poems are *Stopping by Woods on a Snowy Evening, Mending Wall, Nothing Gold Can Stay,* and *Birches.*

A natural symbol for Robert Frost is something frosty. Since all these poem titles refer to concrete things, making symbols for them is not difficult. The following figure is one possible mnemonigram for this group portrait.

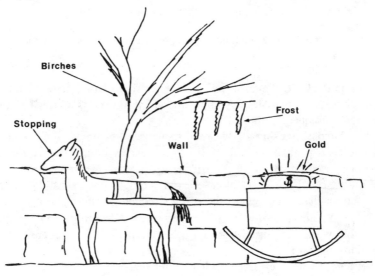

*Exercise 3-8*

Develop a symbol for each of the types of igneous rocks listed below. (The first has been done as an example.) Combine the symbol for igneous and for the four rock types in a group portrait. On separate paper, write a description of your group portrait or draw a mnemonigram.

| NAME | SYMBOL |
|------|--------|
| Igneous | |
| | |
| Gabbro | Someone gabbing |
| Granite | |
| Basalt | |
| Rhyolite | |

To check your recall, turn to page 91 at least 15 minutes after *rehearsing* the associations from memory.

**Using Peg Words.** A peg-word list is a series of names for concrete objects that you can easily recall in correct order. When you have a group of items to remember, you can:

- Develop a symbol for each item; then
- Associate each symbol with one of the peg words

RHYMING PEG WORDS

| | | | |
|---|---|---|---|
| 1 GUN | | 11 A LEVER | |
| 2 SHOE | | 12 ELF | |
| 3 TREE | | 13 THIRSTING | |
| 4 DOOR | | 14 FORKING | |
| 5 HIVE | | 15 FIXING | |
| 6 STICKS | | 16 SITTING | |
| 7 HEAVEN | | 17 SEVERING | |
| 8 GATE | | 18 AIDING | |
| 9 LINE | | 19 KNIGHTING | |
| 10 HEN | | 20 TWINTY | |

Over the years, many peg-word systems have been developed. The figure on the preceding page shows a relatively simple, easy-to-learn rhyming system with 20 peg words. (Lists to be learned seldom have more than 20 items.)

### Exercise 3-9

Complete this exercise after you have learned at least the first seven peg words. Develop symbols for each level of classification used to classify plants and animals. Associate each symbol with its peg word. The first two have been completed as examples.

| PEG WORD | NAME | SYMBOL | PICTURE |
|---|---|---|---|
| 1. Gun | Kingdom | Crown | Gun shooting crown off someone's head |
| 2. Shoe | Phylum | File 'em (file cabinet) | Shoe in a file drawer |
| 3. Tree | Class | | |
| 4. Door | Order | | |
| 5. Hive | Family | | |
| 6. Sticks | Genus | | |
| 7. Heaven | Species | | |

To check your recall, turn to page 91 at least 15 minutes after *rehearsing* the associations from memory.

**Other Peg-Word Systems.** One problem with peg-word systems is that you cannot effectively use the same set of peg words to learn two groups of information simultaneously. The result is a kind of mental double exposure; you begin to confuse the two symbols that relate to the same peg word.

One solution is to have several peg-word systems available. Any group of items that you already know in a particular sequence can be used as a peg-word system. Some examples are:

- Letters of the alphabet, with each representing an object shaped like the letter (A = pyramid, B = bow, C = moon, D = harp, etc.)
- Colors of the rainbow (red = stop sign, orange = an orange, yellow = sunflower, etc.)

- Pieces of furniture in a room in sequence according to location
- Any sequence of objects, events, etc., with which you are familiar (for example, the sequence of TV shows scheduled for a particular evening)

Thus, you can develop several peg-word systems, using lists you already know. These systems can be used repeatedly, as long as the same list is not used simultaneously for two study tasks.

### Exercise 3-10

On a separate piece of paper, develop a new peg-word system with at least ten peg words.

**Using Linking Symbols.** Another way to avoid the "double exposure" problem of peg words is to use the linking-symbol method. The steps are:

1. Develop a symbol for each item (the same as when using a peg-word system).
2. Also develop a trigger symbol to start the sequence.
3. Associate the trigger symbol with the symbol for the first item.
4. Associate the first symbol with the second, the second with the third, and so forth.

In other words, you develop a chain of associations that link the symbol for each item with the following symbol. Suppose in biology you want to remember, in correct sequence, the layers of a tree trunk or branch. From the center outward they are:

| NAME | SYMBOL | PICTURE LINKING SYMBOL WITH PREVIOUS SYMBOL |
| --- | --- | --- |
| (trigger) | Tree | — |
| Pith | Pith helmet (safari helmet) | Tree falling on pith helmet |
| Xylem | "X" railroad sign | Pith helmet hanging on "X" sign |
| Cambium | Can (container) | "X" sign squashing can |
| Phloem | Flowing river | Can floating on river |

| NAME | SYMBOL | PICTURE LINKING SYMBOL WITH PREVIOUS SYMBOL |
|------|--------|---------------------------------------------|
| Cortex | Court (judicial) | River flowing through court |
| Lenticel | Lint | Court judge with lint on coat |
| Cork | Cork (stopper) | Lint pile with cork in it |

When you want to recall the sequence, simply visualize a tree, the trigger symbol. The tree will remind you of a pith helmet, and so forth.

### *Exercise 3-11*

Use the linking-symbol method to learn the sequence of planets.

| NAME | SYMBOL | PICTURE LINKING SYMBOL WITH PREVIOUS SYMBOL |
|------|--------|---------------------------------------------|
| (*trigger*) | Sun | — |
| Mercury | | |
| Venus | | |
| Earth | | |
| Mars | | |
| Jupiter | | |
| Saturn | | |
| Uranus | | |
| Neptune | | |
| Pluto | | |

To check your recall, turn to page 91 at least 15 minutes after *rehearsing* the associations from memory.

**Using a Story.** The story method is similar to the linking-symbol approach. In both cases, ideas are being linked together in a chain. But with the story method, you develop a plot that makes sense.

For example, suppose you want to remember that John Steinbeck wrote:

| TITLE | SYMBOL |
|---|---|
| Of Mice and Men | Mice |
| The Chrysanthemums | Chrysanthemums |
| The Grapes of Wrath | Grapes |
| Tortilla Flat | Tortillas |
| East of Eden | East |
| The Winter of Our Discontent | Winter |

STORY: The glass *stein* (Steinbeck) sits on a table. Someone pours *grape* juice into the stein and eats a stack of *tortillas*. Then s/he puts a *chrysanthemum* in her/his lapel and walks outside, which is a *winter* scene. *Mice* scurry across the snow. S/he walks off into the rising (*east*) sun.

### Exercise 3-12

Suppose you want to remember the four basic universals of economics present in all economic organizations. Develop symbols for each and link them together with a story. (Use separate paper.)

| ECONOMIC UNIVERSAL | SYMBOL |
|---|---|
| Dividing up scarce resources | |
| Distributing goods and services | |
| Providing economic stability and security | |
| Providing continued economic growth | |

To check your recall, turn to page 91 at least 15 minutes after *rehearsing* the story and the meaning of each symbol from memory.

**Using Key-Letter Sentences.** To use this method you construct a sentence in which the first letter of each word is the same as the first letter of the word, idea, event, etc., you want to remember. If possible, the content of the sentence should be related to the information you want to remember. For example, suppose you want to remember that the visible colors of the spectrum (as seen in a rainbow) are red, orange, yellow, green, blue, indigo, and violet, in that order. You could develop a sentence like:

Rainbows only yield gold bricks in visions.

This method should be used with caution, however. In the example above, recalling the colors from single letters is relatively easy because only a limited number of color names are available to choose from. But in other cases, you may find it difficult to recall a key word from a single-letter cue.

### *Exercise 3-13*

The average composition of crystal rocks, in order of decreasing percentages, is: oxygen, silicon, aluminum, sodium, calcium, iron, magnesium, and potassium. On a separate piece of paper develop one or more key-letter sentences to remind you of this sequence.

To check your recall, turn to page 91 at least 15 minutes after *rehearsing* this information from memory.

**Using Acronyms.** An acronym (AK-row-nim) is one or more words or nonsense syllables in which each letter represents a separate piece of information to be remembered. One example is the acronym R.A.V.E. used to help you remember the four key memory methods. (Do you remember what they are? If not, turn to page 15.)

An acronym well known to science students is ROY G. BIV, representing the colors of the visible light spectrum, mentioned on page 39.

Most acronyms deal with nonsequential information. Sequential information seldom happens to form an acronym in the way that the colors of the light spectrum coincidentally form ROY G. BIV. Usually you have to juggle the words until you find a sequence that can be turned into an acronym. To make an acronym, you may sometimes need to replace a word with a similar-meaning word that has a different first letter. If you cannot find a way to turn a group of items into an acronym, you will have to use one of the other mnemonic strategies.

Acronyms have the same potential problem as key-letter sentences. Since you have only a single letter as a cue for each item, you sometimes may have trouble remembering what the letter stands for.

Here is an example from chemistry of using an acronym. Suppose you want to remember that the halogens are the highly reactive nonmetals: fluorine, chlorine, bromine, and iodine. First, you might select *halo* as the symbol for *halogens*. By juggling the initial letters of the elements you come up with the acronym C + FIB. To associate the elements with the term *halogen,* you contrast a *halo* with a *fib.* You also visualize someone *reacting strongly* (highly reactive) to a *fib.*

### *Exercise 3-14*

On a separate piece of paper, develop an acronym to help you remember that the earth's atmosphere contains nitrogen, oxygen, argon, carbon dioxide, and water vapor. (You will have to rearrange the sequence to make an acronym.)

To check your recall, turn to page 91 at least 15 minutes after *rehearsing* the information from memory.

**Remembering Formulas.** Being able to remember key formulas is an important memory task in subjects like mathematics, physics, and chemistry. Ideally, you should be able to construct a formula through your knowledge of the underlying concepts. But under the pressure of an exam situation, you often do not have time to derive the needed formula. Mnemonic techniques can help you quickly recall it.

Formulas are one of the most challenging areas in which to apply mnemonic techniques. You need to be extremely flexible, using your imagination to its fullest. Often you will be combining artificial associations with logical and/or natural ones. (See pages 16–17.)

Suppose you want to remember that the formula for mass density is

$$p = \frac{m}{v}$$

where $p$ = mass density, $m$ = mass, and $v$ = volume. That $m$ stands for mass is easy to remember since *mass* begins with an $m$. $V$ could stand for velocity, but that possibility would make little sense in a formula for density. To remember that $p$ stands for density, you might think of a word beginning with $p$ that reminds you of density—*packed,* for example.

Using a logical association, you might think to yourself that having *volume* in the denominator makes sense because the more space (volume) something occupies, the less dense it would be.

To develop an artificial association for remembering that density = $m/v$, you need to use your imagination. For example, $m$ resembles eyebrows and $v$ a smile, so you could visualize

and think that this person looks very "dense."

42

Another example, from chemistry, is the equation for photosynthesis.

$$6CO_2 + 6H_2O + \text{ENERGY} \longrightarrow C_6H_{12}O_6 + 6O_2$$

First, the left side: To remember $CO_2$, $H_2O$, and ENERGY, you might think to yourself that plants need carbon dioxide, water, and sunlight to carry out photosynthesis (natural association). To remember the sixes, think of six = sticks (peg-word) and visualize a stick in a pool of water ($H_2O$) surrounded by a gas ($CO_2$) (artificial association).

Next, the right side: $C_6H_{12}O_6$ is glucose, a sugar. (Thinking of "C and H Sugar," a brand name, may help you remember this.) C H O + O are the first four letters of the word *choose*. Visualize someone *choosing* sugar, maybe cubes of which are hanging from a tree (photosynthesis).

Three of the four letters on the right side have sixes. Remember that a six *precedes* all parts of the equation except glucose. In glucose, a six is on each side of twelve, the sum of six plus six.

The $O_2$ is easy to remember, since that is oxygen, a byproduct of photosynthesis.

This description of the associations may seem lengthy, but only a few minutes are needed to develop them. As these two examples show, there is no single method for remembering formulas. Flexibility is required to take advantage of whatever associations you can make in each case.

### Exercise 3-15

Develop a mnemonic strategy for remembering each of the following formulas.

1. The area of a triangle = $\frac{1}{2}bh$ where $b$ = base and $h$ = height.

2. $3H_2SO_4$ + $H_2S \longrightarrow 4SO_2 + 4H_2O$
   sulfuric acid    hydrogen sulfide*    sulfur dioxide    water

   *A gas having the foul smell of rotten eggs

3. $w = mg$, where $w$ = weight, $m$ = mass, and $g$ = the acceleration due to gravity.

4. The area of a trapezoid = $\frac{1}{2}h(b_1 + b_2)$. (See following page.)

To test your recall, turn to page 91 at least 15 minutes after *rehearsing* the material from memory.

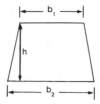

## TWO-WAY SYSTEMS

You've learned how to remember a group of items, such as books written by a particular author. However, in your studies you often will *also* need to remember one or more details about each item in a group. You can accomplish this task by linking these details to the same symbol used in the group system. If only one detail must be remembered, a picture can be developed as shown in the section "Remembering Pairs." If more than one detail must be recalled, the group portrait, linking-symbol, or story method is usually better. The following figure illustrates how a two-way system works.

*Group of item symbols*
*linked by group portrait,*
*peg words, linking symbol,*     *Details branching off*
*linking story, etc.*     *each item symbol*

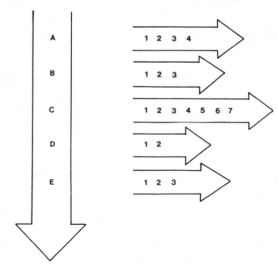

For instance, on pages 37 and 38 is an example showing the layers found in a woody system. In the example, you are told how to remember the sequence by use of the linking-symbol method.

Suppose you also need to remember that new cells for increasing the plant's thickness are developed in the *cambium* area. The symbol being used for cambium is a can. You could link these two by visualizing a can growing increasingly thicker. Another detail: The *xylem* layer is thickest during a wet season. To remember this fact you could imagine a railroad sign (the symbol for xylem) partly submerged in water.

The potential for this kind of branching is tremendous. If you wish, you can have a large system of information stored in your memory for easy recall. To rehearse it, you simply review the information piece by piece in your mind—without having to refer to notes or a textbook. That's confidence!

### *Exercise 3-16*

Below is a sequence of major events in the early federal period of U.S. history. Details related to each major event are provided. On separate paper, develop a two-way system using whichever mnemonic strategies you feel would be most effective. For example, you might use a peg-word system for the main events and group portraits for the details.

Symbols are provided for the first set as examples.

| SEQUENCE OF MAIN EVENTS | DETAILS RELATED TO EACH MAIN EVENT |
|---|---|
| Hamilton's financial plan (symbol: ham with "$" on it) | Government paid debts (symbol: bill with "Paid" written on it) |
| | Government encouraged economic expansion (symbol: gears, representing industry) |
| | Government authorized use of coins, paper money (symbol: pile of coins) |

| SEQUENCE OF MAIN EVENTS | DETAILS RELATED TO EACH MAIN EVENT |
| --- | --- |
| Rise of political parties | Hamilton's Federalist party: strong central government; manufacturing interests |
| | Jefferson's Antifederalist party: limited federal government; farming interests |
| Louisiana Purchase | Greatest land deal in U.S. history |
| War of 1812 | Some causes— |
| | Violations of U.S. neutrality |
| | British forced U.S. sailors into British navy |

To test your recall, turn to page 93 at least 15 minutes after *rehearsing* the information from memory. For another example of using a two-way system, see pages 53 and 54.

## REMEMBERING RULES, PROCEDURES, AND PRINCIPLES

In many courses, you sometimes need to remember important rules, procedures, and principles. To remember these pieces of information, you probably will find yourself combining logical, natural, and/or artificial associations (pages 16–17).

Suppose you want to remember Archimedes' principle: "A body immersed in a liquid is lifted by a force equal to the weight of the fluid displaced by the body." If you are familiar with the story of how Archimedes discovered this principle while taking a bath, that knowledge would be a useful natural association.

Other natural associations might be examples of cases where Archimedes' principle applies; for example, when a fish expands itself with air, it displaces more water and therefore becomes more buoyant. For an artificial association you might visualize an *ark* (for Archimedes) being pushed upward by a force equal to the water it displaces.

### *Exercise 3-17*

Develop a mnemonic strategy for remembering each of the following.

1. When adding two square roots, combine the numbers under the radical ($\sqrt{\phantom{x}}$) before computing the square root.

2. The earth's seasons occur because its axis is not perpendicular to its orbit. Instead, the earth's rotational axis is tilted.

3. An exterior angle of a triangle is equal to the sum of the opposite interior angles. For example, angle ABC = angle BCD + angle BDC.

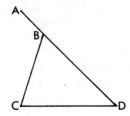

4. The indefinite pronoun *each* takes a singular verb: "Each of the boys *is* (not *are*) going separately."

To test your recall turn to page 93 at least 15 minutes after *rehearsing* the material from memory.

# Part Two
# Applying The Methods

Part Two

- Explains how to deal with special memory challenges in major school subjects
- Provides exercises classified by subject area

CAREFULLY STUDY ALL OF PART ONE
BEFORE WORKING WITH THE MATERIAL IN PART TWO.

The following process is recommended:

- Turn to the section you wish to study.
- Develop mnemonic strategies as indicated in the section. If you need to refresh yourself on a mnemonic technique, turn to the page given in parentheses with the word *Method*.
- Most of the exercises in Part Two suggest a 30-minute delay before you take the memory test. To test your long-term memory, you may want to retake the test 24 or 48 hours later.
- If you miss an item on the test, ask yourself why. Did you follow the mnemonic suggestions? If you visualized a mental image, was it done vividly? Did you *rehearse* the associations from memory?
- Also, note what you did *right* when you do remember an item.

# 4

# REMEMBERING THE SOCIAL SCIENCES

## REMEMBERING SOCIOLOGY

Sociology is the study of human interactions — the structure of social relationships. Sociologists examine interactions in groups: families, gangs, clubs, companies, cities, regions, nations, and so forth.

Some common memory tasks in sociology are:

- Remembering terms and their meanings
- Remembering sociologists and their experiments or theories
- Remembering lists of categories, classifications, etc.

### *Exercise 4-1*

Develop mnemonic strategies for learning the definitions of the following terms. (Method: pages 26–27.)

1. *Acculturation.* The process whereby the culture and behavior of one group is adopted by another group.
2. *Anomie* (AN-uh-mee). A condition in which members of a society or group have a weakened respect for some of the norms.
3. *Caste.* A class or social group whose membership is determined by birth and whose boundaries are rigidly fixed.
4. *Ethnocentrism.* The belief that the behavior and culture of one's own group is superior to that of others.
5. *Folk society.* An underdeveloped, isolated society that is small, intimate, and very cohesive.

49

6. *Diffusion*. The spread of traits from one culture to another.
7. *Endogamy*. Marriage within a certain group.
8. *Polyandry*. One woman married to several men at one time.

To test your recall of these definitions, turn to page 93 at least 30 minutes after *rehearsing* the items from memory.

### Exercise 4-2

Develop mnemonic strategies for linking the sociologists below with their contributions to sociology. (Method: pages 23–25.)

1. *Durkheim*. Introduced the concept of anomie. (See definition of *anomie* in Exercise 4-1.)
2. *Meltzer*. Concerned about the effects of isolation on prisoners.
3. *Cooley*. Conceived the idea of the "looking-glass self," having 3 stages: perception, interpretation, and response.
4. *Fischer*. Developed a "subcultural theory" to explain urban behavior: An urban society has numerous subcultures.
5. *Money*. Studied sex roles and stereotyping.
6. *Sorokin*. Suggested that societies have "sensate" and "ideational" cycles.

To test your recall, turn to page 93 at least 30 minutes after *rehearsing* the material from memory.

### Exercise 4-3

Develop a mnemonic strategy for remembering the five characteristics that distinguish an industrial society from a youth counterculture. (Method: pages 32–42.)

#### Industrial Ethics

1. Hard Work
2. Control over nature
3. Rational approach
4. Future oriented
5. Self-reliance and individualism

To test your recall, turn to page 93 at least 30 minutes after *rehearsing* the material from memory.

## Exercise 4-4

Develop a mnemonic strategy for remembering the six major ways people are influenced. (Method: pages 32 – 42.)

1. Information
2. Coercion (force)
3. Referent (modeling desired behavior)
4. Expertise
5. Reward
6. Legitimacy (you ought to do it, etc.)

Test your recall by turning to page 95 at least 30 minutes after *rehearsing* the material from memory.

## Exercise 4-5

Develop a mnemonic strategy for remembering four kinds of groupings distinguished by Blumer and the details of each. (Method: pages 43 – 45.)

1. *Acting crowd.* A temporary grouping that has an *aggressive* goal, such as taking over a building in protest.
2. *Expressive crowd.* A temporary grouping without a single goal. Each individual engages in his or her own expressive actions, such as laughing or dancing.
3. *Mass.* A large number of people who react to a common stimulus (for example, a gold rush) but act individually.
4. *Public.* A vaguely defined group of people who, for a time, confront, discuss, and disagree about a particular issue. The grouping is temporary and there is no feeling of common identity.

To test your recall, turn to page 95 at least 30 minutes after *rehearsing* this material from memory.

## REMEMBERING HISTORY

History is the study of the recorded events of the human race. Some common memory tasks in history are:

- Remembering names of historical figures and what they accomplished
- Remembering names of and details about battles, wars, treaties, and other events
- Remembering dates and what happened (although stressed less today)
- Remembering sequences of events and details

When you are studying history, markers often are useful. These can be reigns of rulers, names and dates of major wars, inventions, treaties, and the like. For a particular period, build an outline showing these bench marks in chronological order. Memorize the dates of the events on this outline. Then you will have a series of useful reference points with which you can associate other historical information you want to remember.

### Exercise 4-6

Develop mnemonic strategies to associate the historical figures below with the details related to them. (Method: pages 23–25.)

1. *Randolph.* Virginia congressman who strongly opposed war with England (War of 1812).
2. *Hull.* American general during the American Revolution and War of 1812. During the latter war, he surrendered his army without a fight.
3. *Bingham.* Congressman and painter of political pictures.
4. *Seward.* Secretary of state who purchased Alaska from Russia.
5. *Woodhull.* First woman candidate for president.
6. *Tilden.* Presidential candidate who won the election but was defeated in the electoral college by corrupt methods.
7. *Hill.* American railroad tycoon who hoped to build a worldwide American railroad chain.
8. *Wheeler.* Montana senator who opposed the Lend-Lease plan to deliver weapons to Hilter's foes.

To test your recall, turn to page 95 at least 30 minutes after *rehearsing* the material from memory.

## Exercise 4-7

Develop a mnemonic strategy for remembering the events and dates given below. (Method: pages 29–31.)

1. *1804*. Aaron Burr kills Hamilton in a duel.
2. *1893*. Congress holds an emergency session to discuss repeal of the Silver Act.
3. *1869*. The Pacific railroad is completed.
4. *1921*. The Panama Canal is officially declared finished.
5. *1920*. American women gain the right to vote.
6. *1881*. President Garfield is fatally shot.
7. *1931*. Japan seizes Manchuria, ending a period of relative peace.
8. *1825*. The Erie Canal is officially opened.

To test your recall, turn to page 95 at least 30 minutes after *rehearsing* the material from memory.

## Exercise 4-8

Develop a mnemonic strategy for remembering that Jefferson had three primary goals when writing the Declaration of Independence. (Method: pages 32–42.)

1. To present a theory of government.
2. To prove to foreign governments that America was determined to be free.
3. To use as a propaganda weapon.

*Suggestion:* Since there are only four items, including Jefferson, you might want to develop a symbol for each and create a group portrait.

To test your recall, turn to page 95 at least 30 minutes after *rehearsing* the material from memory.

## Exercise 4-9

Here is a chance to develop a two-way system (Method: pages 43–45.) Below are listed six English kings, in correct sequence of succession. Some key details are included about each king. Develop a mnemonic strategy to remember the sequence and details.

*Suggestion:* The kings' names present a special challenge, since there are two different Edwards and three different Henries included. One solution would be to develop a symbol for the name and combine it with the peg-word symbol that corresponds to the number (see pages 35–37). For example, the symbol for Edward II might combine *head* (rhymes with *Ed*) and *shoe* (peg-word symbol for *two*). Edward III would translate into *head* + *tree*.

The steps, then, would be to tie the kings together and then link details to each king. For example, Edward II was imprisoned, so you might visualize your symbol for him associated with a prison.

1. *Edward II.* Weak. Barons revolted. His queen had him imprisoned and murdered.
2. *Edward III.* Needed money to fight French. House of Commons began to control finances. Economic crisis, partly due to plague.
3. *Richard II.* Harshly suppressed a peasant revolt. Defeated by Duke of Gloucester. Richard later arrested Gloucester.
4. *Henry IV.* Had to deal with many rebellions. Parliament gained more financial power.
5. *Henry V.* Won great victories in France, but neglected England. Died young.
6. *Henry VI.* Was mentally unstable as he grew up.

To test your recall, turn to page 97 at least 30 minutes after *rehearsing* the material from memory.

### Exercise 4-10

Develop a mnemonic strategy for remembering, in sequence, some major events of the Civil War and some key details about each. (Method: pages 43–45.)

1. *Fort Sumter.* The Union fort, under Anderson, falls to Beauregard. War is declared.
2. *First Battle of Bull Run.* Generals Johnson and Jackson defeat the Union, under McDowell.
3. *Shenandoah Valley.* Jackson ("Stonewall") wins many victories, preventing the Union's McClellan from getting reinforcements.
4. *Seven Days' Battle.* Lee forces McClellan to retreat.
5. *Second Battle of Bull Run.* Union badly defeated while led by Pope.
6. *Battle of Antietam.* McClellan forces Lee to retreat, but fails to pursue him. Very bloody battle.

7. *Emancipation Proclamation*. After the Antietam victory, Lincoln announces intention to free slaves in Confederate States.
8. *Fredericksburg*. Burnside makes six unsuccessful charges against Lee's forces.
9. *Chancellorsville*. The Union's Hooker is badly defeated, but Stonewall Jackson is killed, and the South has a heavy toll of dead.
10. *Gettysburg*. Lee gambles on invading the North and loses to Meade.

To test your recall, turn to page 97 at least 30 minutes after *rehearsing* the material from memory.

## REMEMBERING ART HISTORY

Art history deals with the evolution of human creative efforts, from the first attempts at carving and wall painting to the most modern works of art. Some of the main categories in art history are drawing and painting, crafts, sculpture, and architecture.

Some common memory tasks in art history are:

- Remembering names of artists, architects, etc., and their works
- Associating artists, etc., with details about their style, influence, and so forth
- Remembering technical terms and their definitions
- Linking dates with key events
- Remembering characteristics of a period (such as the Renaissance)

### *Exercise 4-11*

Develop a mnemonic strategy for remembering each artist and a representative work of his. (Method: pages 23–25.)

1. *Rouault* (Roo-OH). "The Old Clown" (painting)
2. *Picasso*. "The Blue Boy" (painting)
3. *Marc*. "The Three Horses" (painting)
4. *Weber*. "The Broken Tree" (painting)
5. *Graves*. "Wounded Gull" (painting)
6. *Brancusi*. "Bird in Space" (sculpture)
7. *Marini*. "Horse and Rider" (sculpture)

To test your recall, turn to page 97 at least 30 minutes after *rehearsing* the material from memory.

56

## Exercise 4-12

Develop a mnemonic strategy for remembering each of the terms below. (Method: pages 26–27.)

1. *Minaret* (min-uh-RET). Slender tower attached to a mosque (mosque: Moslem house of worship).
2. *Pendentive*. Triangular section of vaulting used to support a dome.
3. *Chiaroscuro* (key-are-uh-SKOOR-oh). Use of light and dark in a painting.
4. *Diptych* (DIP-tick). Picture or series of pictures on two hinged tablets.
5. *Icon.* A picture of a sacred Christian personage.

To test your recall, turn to page 97 at least 30 minutes after *rehearsing* the material from memory.

## Exercise 4-13

Develop mnemonic strategies for remembering some major characteristics of impressionist and expressionist painters and the names of some artists in each group. (Method: pages 32–42.)

*Suggestion:* First develop symbols for the two schools of painting, impressionism (an imprint, someone acting impressed, etc.) and expressionism. Also develop symbols for the other information. Then, link each set of characteristics to the appropriate school. In a separate association, connect the names to their schools. Since none of the information is sequential, you can use any of the grouping methods.

### IMPRESSIONISTS

| Characteristics | Artists |
| --- | --- |
| 1. Technique very important | 1. Pissarro |
| 2. Very colorful | 2. Monet (mow-NAY) |
| 3. Tiny dots sometimes used | 3. Renoir |
| 4. Concerned about effects of light | |

### EXPRESSIONISTS

| Characteristics | Artists |
| --- | --- |
| 1. Did not imitate nature | 1. Cezanne (say-ZON) |
| 2. Usually dynamic | 2. van Gogh (van GO) |
| 3. *Sometimes* abstract | 3. Gauguin (go-GAN) |

To test your recall, turn to page 99 at least 30 minutes after *rehearsing* the material from memory.

## REMEMBERING PSYCHOLOGY

Psychology deals with the study of human behavior. While sociology concentrates on the interaction among people in groups, psychology focuses more on individual behavior. However, the two disciplines do overlap.

Some common memory tasks in psychology are:

- Remembering names of psychologists and details about them —their work, their theories, etc.
- Remembering psychological terms and their definitions
- Remembering lists of categories and classifications
- Remembering the history of how a theory was developed, what evidence supports or refutes it, etc.

### *Exercise 4-14*

Develop mnemonic strategies for learning the definitions of the following terms. (Method: pages 26–27.)

1. *Double bind.* When a person is told one thing while simultaneously receiving signals that the opposite is true.
2. *Imprinting.* A learned attachment formed during a particular period in an organism's life.
3. *Heuristics.* In computer problem solving, a procedure which has often worked before and probably will work again.
4. *Hyperphagia.* Excessive, chronic overeating caused by a lesion in the brain.
5. *Syndrome.* A pattern of symptoms that tend to go together.
6. *Aphasia.* A language disorder caused by a lesion in the brain.
7. *Cones.* Visual receptors that respond to more intense light and give rise to sensations of color.
8. *Displacement.* A concept in psychoanalytic theory which says that when an impulse is blocked, the person may use a more available outlet. (For example, child hits the dog if cannot hit the parent.)

To test your recall, turn to page 99 at least 30 minutes after *rehearsing* this material from memory.

58

## Exercise 4-15

Develop mnemonic strategies for remembering the psychologists below and the details about each. (Method: pages 23–25.)

1. *McClelland.* Has studied cultural factors in the development of the motivation to achieve.
2. *Premack.* Has worked with chimpanzees to study language acquisition.
3. *Hering.* Nineteenth-century psychophysiologist who studied properties of vision.
4. *Duncker.* Performed a classic study on problem solving.
5. *Weber.* Developed a formula for measuring differences in sensory intensity (light, sounds, etc.).
6. *Galton.* Pioneer in the study of individual differences.
7. *Rosch.* Developed the *prototype* theory of meaning: People have in their memories prototypes against which they compare members of each class.
8. *Tinbergen.* Has studied instinctive behavior in animals. Found that some instinctive behavior aids survival.

To test your recall, turn to page 99 at least 30 minutes after *rehearsing* the material from memory.

## Exercise 4-16

Develop a mnemonic strategy for remembering the stages in Maslow's hierarchy of needs and the details on each stage. Also, associate Maslow's name with "hierarchy of needs." (Methods: pages 23–25, 43–45.)

| Hierarchy Levels (Lowest to Highest) | If Needs Met at This Level |
|---|---|
| 1. Physiological needs | Comfort, sense of well being |
| 2. Safety needs | Security, comfort |
| 3. Love needs | Warm feelings, free expression of emotions |
| 4. Esteem needs | Confidence, self-respect |
| 5. Self-actualization needs | Work, creative, positive thinking |

To test your recall, turn to page 99 at least 30 minutes after *rehearsing* the material from memory.

## *Exercise 4-17*

Develop a mnemonic strategy for remembering Jean Piaget's (pee-ah-ZHAY) theory of the stages children pass through. Also, link Piaget's name with his theory.

*Suggestion:* Develop a two-way system for the sequence of stages and the details of each (page 43). For ages, you could use peg words (for example, two years old = shoe) (page 35) and associate each with the symbol for the stage.

1. *Sensorimotor period.* (By two years old.) Children are aware of themselves as separate beings from the rest of the world. They have developed a sense of *object permanence,* which means they realize that an object that is hidden still exists.
2. *Preoperational period.* (By seven years old.) Children have learned to use language to communicate. They understand the principle of *conservation of items.* For example, they realize that if water is poured from a wide glass into a narrow glass, the amount remains the same, even though the water level in the narrow glass is higher.
3. *Concrete operations.* (By eleven years old.) Children develop the idea of *conservation of mass, weight, and volume.* When an object is broken into parts, the total weight is the same. Six dots are six dots, no matter how much space is between them. Children are now mentally ready to learn simple arithmetic.
4. *Formal operations.* (Eleven years old and older.) Children are able to do *abstract thinking* instead of only concrete thinking. They can deal with more philosophical questions such as "What is justice?" and "Is there a God?"

To test your recall, turn to page 99 at least 30 minutes after *rehearsing* the material from memory.

**5**

# REMEMBERING THE PHYSICAL SCIENCES

## REMEMBERING CHEMISTRY

Chemistry is the study of the composition, structure, properties, and reactions of matter. It deals especially with atomic and molecular systems. There is some overlap between chemistry and physics.

Some common memory tasks in chemistry are:

- Remembering terms and their definitions
- Remembering concepts
- Remembering chemical equations and how to derive them
- Remembering properties of matter and how different materials interact
- Remembering the sequence of steps required to achieve a certain reaction

*Learning by Doing.* Chemistry involves a lot of computations. With chemistry, math, and other computational subjects, *practice* is an essential part of the memory process. Mnemonic methods are very helpful, but nothing takes the place of working the problems.

### *Exercise 5-1*

Develop a mnemonic strategy for remembering each of the following chemical equations. (Method: pages 41–42.)

1. $SO_2CL_2 + 2H_2O \longrightarrow H_2SO_4 + 2HCL$
$$\text{\textit{sulfuric acid}}$$

60

2.  $$2H_2S + 3O_2 \longrightarrow 2H_2O + 2SO_2$$
    *hydrogen*
    *sulfide*

3.  $$2NH_3 + 3CL_2 \longrightarrow N_2 + 6HCL$$
    *ammonia*

4.  $$3N_2O_4 + 2H_2O \longrightarrow 4HNO_3 + 2NO$$
    *nitric*
    *acid*

To test your recall, turn to page 101 at least 30 minutes after *rehearsing* these equations from memory.

### Exercise 5-2

Develop a mnemonic strategy for remembering the elemental symbols that are not easily related to the elements they represent (that is, that do not being with the same letters as the element). (Method: pages 26–27.) The first three have been done as examples.

| Element | Symbol |
|---|---|
| 1. Copper | Cu |
| *Association:* | Copper colored hair is cute. |
| 2. Gold | Au |
| *Association:* | The sun is gold in August. |
| 3. Iron | Fe |
| *Association:* | She irons for a fee. |
| 4. Lead | Pb |
| 5. Mercury | Hg |
| 6. Potassium | K |
| 7. Silver | Ag |
| 8. Sodium | Na |
| 9. Tin | Sn |
| 10. Tungsten | W |

To test your recall, turn to page 101 at least 30 minutes after *rehearsing* these equations from memory.

62

## Exercise 5-3

Develop a mnemonic strategy for remembering some properties of alpha, beta, and gamma rays. A solution for alpha rays has been provided as an example.

1. Alpha rays
   Mass = 4

   Charge = $2^+$

   *Symbol:* Alfalfa plant
   4 = T (number-letter key)
   *Picture:* <u>Alfalfa</u> <u>tea</u> on <u>scale</u> (representing mass)
   *Picture:* Someone <u>charging</u> <u>two</u> dollars for <u>alfalfa</u>
   + = plus
   *Association:* <u>Alfalfa</u> is a food, which is a <u>plus</u>.

2. Beta rays
   Mass = 1/1837
   Charge = $1^-$
3. Gamma rays
   Mass = 0
   Charge = 0

To test your recall, turn to page 101 at least 30 minutes after *rehearsing* the material from memory.

## Exercise 5-4

Develop a mnemonic strategy for remembering the Atomic Mass Units (a.m.u.) of some common elements. (Method: pages 29–32.) A solution is provided for the first one as an example.

1. Aluminum = 27 a.m.u.   *Symbol:* can
   2 = N, 7 = F (number-letter key)
   *Association:* A <u>n</u>early <u>f</u>ull <u>aluminum</u> <u>can</u>

2. Carbon = 12 a.m.u.
3. Helium = 4 a.m.u.
4. Hydrogen = 1 a.m.u.
5. Iron = 56 a.m.u.
6. Oxygen = 16 a.m.u.

To test your recall, turn to page 101 at least 30 minutes after *rehearsing* the information from memory.

## Exercise 5-5

Develop a mnemonic strategy for remembering the electron dot formulas for the first 20 elements. (Method: pages 26–27.)

*Suggestion:* You might use peg words (page 35) to provide symbols for each dot formula (for example, one dot = gun, two = shoe, etc.). Then, use a group memory method (group portrait, etc.) to link a symbol for a dot formula to symbols you have developed for the elements having that formula. You would not want to use the peg word system used for the dot formulas, however, because of possible confusion.

| 1 | 2 | 3 | 4 | 5 | 6 | 7 | |
|---|---|---|---|---|---|---|---|
| • | • • | • <br> • • | • • | • • <br> • • | • • <br> • <br> • | • • <br> • • <br> • | *Noble Gases* |
| Hydrogen | | | | | | | Helium |
| Lithium | Beryllium | Boron | Carbon | Nitrogen | Oxygen | Fluorine | |
| Sodium | Magnesium | Aluminum | Silicon | Phosphorus | Sulfur | Chlorine | Argon |
| Potassium | Calcium | | | | | | |

To test your recall, turn to page 101 at least 30 minutes after *rehearsing* the material from memory.

## REMEMBERING PHYSICS

Physics is the study of matter and energy and the interactions between the two. Fields include acoustics, optics, thermodynamics, and nuclear physics. There is some overlap between physics and chemistry.

Some common memory tasks in physics are:

- Remembering terms and their definitions
- Remembering concepts
- Remembering formulas
- Remembering properties of matter and energy

*Learning by Doing.* Physics involves a lot of computations. With physics, math, and other computational subjects, *practice* is an essential part of the memory process. Mnemonic methods are very helpful, but nothing takes the place of working the problems.

## Exercise 5-6

Develop a mnemonic strategy for remembering each of the following physical terms and its definition. (Method: pages 26–27.)

1. *Energy*. The ability to perform work and/or to move objects.
2. *Kinetic energy*. The energy possessed by a moving object.
3. *Potential energy*. The energy possessed by an unstable object at rest.
4. *Temperature*. The measure of the movement of molecules.
5. *Sound*. That which is produced by the mechanical disturbance of a gas, liquid, or solid.
6. *Photon*. A particle of light energy.
7. *Mass*. The quantity of matter, the measure of inertia.
8. *Acceleration*. The rate of change of velocity with time.

To test your recall, turn to page 101 at least 30 minutes after *rehearsing* the material from memory.

## Exercise 5-7

Develop a mnemonic strategy for remembering each of the following formulas. (Method: pages 41–42.)

1. Determine the volume ($V$) of a fluid passing through a pipe with a cross section $A_1$ and more narrow cross section $A_2$, where $p_1 - p_2 =$ the pressure difference and $V_1 =$ the velocity. $K =$ a constant that depends on the pipe and the kind of fluid.

$$V = A_1 A_2 \sqrt{\frac{2(p_1 - p_2)}{p(A_1^2 - A_2^2)}} = K \sqrt{p_1 - p_2}$$

2. Determine the velocity of a bullet, where $h =$ the height a block moves when struck by the bullet, $m_1$ and $m_2 =$ the masses of the bullet and block and $g =$ the acceleration due to gravity.

$$V = \sqrt{2gh}\,(m_1 + m_2)/m_1$$

3. The formula for length contraction is

$$L = \sqrt{1 - V^2/C^2}\,L'$$

where $L'$ = the length observed at rest and $L$ = the length observed in motion.

Test your memory by turning to page 101 at least 30 minutes after *rehearsing* the material from memory.

### Exercise 5-8

Develop a mnemonic strategy for remembering the following conversions. The first one is done for you as an example.

1. One radian = 57.3°. *Radian* sounds like *raid on*. 57.3 translates into SFPM (page 29). So you might memorize the sentence, "Raid on San Francisco public menace."
2. One pound = 453.6 grams
3. One astronomical unit (AU) = $1.496 \times 10^{11}$ meters
4. Degrees Kelvin (°K) = 273.1 + °C

To test your recall, turn to page 103 at least 30 minutes after *rehearsing* the material from memory.

### Exercise 5-9

Develop a mnemonic strategy for remembering the reasons that your weight changes as you move across the earth's surface. (Method: pages 32–42.)

1. A higher altitude causes you to weigh less, since you are further from the earth's center.
2. You weigh less at the equator because the earth's bulge increases your distance from the earth's center.
3. Centrifugal force at the equator works against gravity.
4. You will tend to weigh more where the rocks beneath the earth's surface are unusually heavy.

To test your recall, turn to page 103 at least 30 minutes after *rehearsing* the material from memory.

# 6

## REMEMBERING THE
## LIFE SCIENCES

### REMEMBERING BIOLOGY

Biology is the study of life and life processes. Included is the study of the origin, evolution, and structure of living organisms. Two main divisions of biology are botany (the study of plants) and zoology (the study of animals).

Some common memory tasks in biology are:

- Remembering names of major biologists and their contributions
- Remembering terms and their definitions
- Remembering classifications and descriptions of living organisms

### *Exercise 6-1*

Develop a mnemonic strategy for remembering the following biological terms and their definitions. (Method: pages 26–27.)

1. *Agnaths*. A class of vertebrates without jaws, including some primitive fish.
2. *Anther*. The part of the flower that produces pollen.
3. *Axon*. The nerve fiber that conducts an impulse away from the body of a nerve cell.
4. *Corolla*. The petals of a flower.
5. *Dendrite*. The branching nerve fiber that conducts impulses toward the body of a nerve cell.
6. *Lymph*. A colorless fluid in the body surrounding many cells.
7. *Oogenesis*. The maturation of egg cells.

8. *Symbiosis.* The close living association of two organisms of different species in which both benefit.

To test your recall, turn to page 103 at least 30 minutes after *rehearsing* the information from memory.

### *Exercise 6-2*

Develop a mnemonic strategy for remembering the names of the biologists listed below and their contributions to biology. (Method: pages 23–25.)

1. *Harvey.* Discovered the circulation of blood.
2. *Linnaeus.* Developed a system for classifying organisms.
3. *Lamarck.* Proposed that an organism's acquired characteristics could be inherited. (For example, an animal becomes blinded and therefore its offspring are more likely to be born sightless.)
4. *Watson.* Solved the structure of DNA.
5. *Leeuwenhoek.* Pioneered the use of the microscope.

To test your recall, turn to page 103 at least 30 minutes after *rehearsing* the material from memory.

### *Exercise 6-3*

Develop a mnemonic strategy for remembering the stages of cell division (mitosis) and the details of each. (Method: pages 43–45.)

*Suggestion:* First, develop a symbol for *mitosis.* Then, connect the steps to the term *mitosis,* using one of the group methods appropriate for sequential information.

1. *Prophase.* Chromosomes thicken and the centrosome divides.
2. *Metaphase.* The nuclear membrane disappears and a spindle develops between the two parts of the centrosome. The chromosomes gather on the spindle.
3. *Anaphase.* The spindle divides, splitting each chromosome apart.
4. *Telophase.* The nuclear membranes form, resulting in two new cells.

To test your recall, turn to page 103 at least 30 minutes after *rehearsing* the material from memory.

## *Exercise 6-4*

Develop a mnemonic strategy for remembering, in order of increasing complexity, eleven of the most important animal phyla. Also, remember one or more representative animals in each phyla. (Method: pages 43–45.)

 1. *Porifera.* Sponges
 2. *Coelenterata.* Corals
 3. *Platyhelminthes.* Flatworms
 4. *Nematoda.* Hookworms
 5. *Annelida.* Earthworms
 6. *Bryozoa.* Colonial ocean animals
 7. *Brachiopoda.* Lampshells
 8. *Echinodermata.* Starfish
 9. *Mollusca.* Snails, octopus
10. *Arthropoda.* Crabs, ants, spiders
11. *Chordata.* Sharks, cod, frogs, snakes, birds, mammals

To test your recall, turn to page 105 at least 30 minutes after *rehearsing* the material from memory.

# 7

# REMEMBERING
# MATHEMATICS

Mathematics is the study of numerical systems.
Some common memory tasks in mathematics are:

- Remembering terms and their definitions
- Remembering numbers and what they stand for
- Remembering formulas and what they stand for
- Remembering rules and mathematical procedures

*Learning by Doing.* Mathematics involves a lot of computations. With math, chemistry, and other computational subjects, *practice* is an essential part of the memory process. Mnemonic methods are very helpful, but nothing takes the place of working the problems.

### Exercise 7-1

Develop a mnemonic strategy for remembering each of the following mathematical formulas. (Method: pages 41–42.)

1. If $(x_1, y_1)$ and $(x_2, y_2)$ are two vectors of the space $V$, the distance $d$ and angle $\theta°$ between them are given by:

(a)
$$d = \sqrt{(x_1 - x_2)^2 + (y_1 - y_2)^2}$$

(b)
$$\cos \theta = \frac{x_1 x_2 + y_1 y_2}{\sqrt{x_1^2 + y_1^2} \sqrt{x_2^2 + y_2^2}}$$

2. The general polynomial of degree $n$ is:

$$f(x) = f_n x^n + f_{n-1} x^{n-1} + \ldots$$
$$+ f_1 x + f_0 \ (n \geqslant 0,\ f \neq 0 \ldots.$$

3. When the function for the quotient rule is

$$\frac{f(x)}{g(x)}$$

the derivative is:

$$\frac{g(x)f'(x) - f(x)g'(x)}{\{g(x)\}^2} \ \text{if } g(x) \neq 0$$

To test your recall, turn to page 105 at least 30 minutes after *rehearsing* the material from memory.

### Exercise 7-2

Develop a mnemonic strategy for remembering the names of some lower-case Greek letters commonly used in mathematical notations. The first three are done as examples. (Method: pages 26–27.)

1. $\theta$ *Theta*. Your symbol for theta could be the similar-sounding word *theater*. The Greek letter $\theta$ looks like the film reel on a movie projector used in a theater.
2. $\lambda$ *Lambda* = lamb. The letter $\lambda$ looks like someone running. You could visualize a person chasing a lamb.
3. $\mu$ *mu* = moo (cow). The letter $\mu$ has a "tail" on it that could remind you of a cow.
4. $\nu$ *nu*
5. $\rho$ *rho*
6. $\sigma$ *sigma*
7. $\phi$ *phi*
8. $\psi$ *psi*

To test your recall, turn to page 105 at least 30 minutes after *rehearsing* the material from memory.

## *Exercise 7-3*

Develop a mnemonic strategy for remembering the following mathematical terms and their definitions. (Method: pages 26–27.)

1. *Hypotenuse*. The side of a right triangle opposite the right angle.
2. *Isosceles* triangle. A triangle having two equal sides.
3. *Chord*. The distance across a circle between any two points.
4. *Mean*. Average. The sum of a group of numbers divided by the number of cases.
5. *Mode*. The most frequently occurring score or measure in a group.
6. *Median*. The middle score or number when a group of numbers is arranged in order by size.
7. *X-axis*. The horizontal axis in a coordinate system.
8. *Y-axis*. The vertical axis in a coordinate system.

To test your recall, turn to page 105 at least 30 minutes after *rehearsing* the material from memory.

## *Exercise 7-4*

Develop a mnemonic strategy for remembering each of the following important equivalents.

*Suggestion:* These equivalents can be divided into two main groups, eighths and sixths. For the eighths you could use the rhyming peg-word system for the numerators (page 35). Then, use the number-letter system (page 30) to remember the equivalents. For example,

1. $1/8 = .125$
   1 (in 1/8) = gun (peg word)
   .125 = *l*NS (number-letter key)
   Sample sentence connecting gun with *l*NS; The gun lets noise sound.

For the sixths you could use a different peg-word system (page 36).

2. $3/8 = .375$
3. $5/8 = .625$
4. $7/8 = .875$
5. $1/6 = .16\frac{2}{3}$
6. $5/6 = .83\frac{1}{3}$

To test your recall, turn to page 105 at least 30 minutes after *rehearsing* the material from memory.

### *Exercise 7-5*

Develop a mnemonic strategy for remembering each of the following rules or procedures (Method: pages 45–46.)

1. A quadratic equation is a polynomial whose largest exponent is 2. To solve a quadratic equation:
   a. Move all terms to one side of the equal sign, leaving zero on the other side.
   b. Factor.
   c. Set each factor equal to zero.
   d. Solve each of these equations.
   e. Check by inserting your answer in the original equation.

2. A line parallel to one side of a triangle and cutting the other two sides divides these sides into proportional segments.

3. If two chords intersect within a circle, the product of the segments of one chord is equal to the product of the segments of the other. For example, AE × EB = CE × ED.

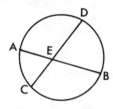

To test your recall, turn to page 107 at least 30 minutes after *rehearsing* this material from memory.

# 8

# REMEMBERING THE LANGUAGES

## REMEMBERING ENGLISH GRAMMAR AND PUNCTUATION

In Chapter 3 mnemonic strategies for vocabulary (pages 26–27) and spelling (pages 28–29) are discussed. English grammar and punctuation are two other areas where mnemonics can be very helpful.

When a rule has some logic to it, a logical association (page 17) can be used. For example, one rule of punctuation states that independent clauses (clauses having subjects and verbs), except when very short, should not be connected by a comma alone. Instead, a semicolon or comma plus conjunction (*and, but,* etc.) should be used. This rule is logical. You might think to yourself, "A comma is too weak to hold two independent clauses together unless the clauses are very short, so a stronger connection is needed." You might even visualize the weak comma being replaced by a stronger connection.

Natural associations (page 16) often can also be used. Since you use language every day, you sometimes can find examples from your own experience to associate with a rule of grammar or punctuation.

### *Exercise 8-1*

Below are listed eight rules of grammar that students often have trouble with. The first four have been completed as examples. Develop mnemonic strategies for remembering the other four.

1. *Rule:* Use a subjective pronoun (for example, *who*) for the subject of a noun clause. Use an objective pronoun (for example, *whom*) for the object of a noun clause.

*Strategy:* Remember that *whom* = *him*. Both are objective, and both end in *m*. For example, "The man *whom* she hated came in." Isolate the clause and change it to the simple sentence "She hated *him*." Him has an *m* like *whom*, so you know *whom* is correct. Contrast that sentence with "Tom is the boy *who* I think will succeed." After changing the clause to "I think *he* will succeed," you know *who* is correct because *he* is used instead of *him*.

2. *Rule:* A pronoun being used as an object must be objective in form. Compound objects (such as *Tom and me*) are especially confusing. For example, "The policeman called to Tom and me (not *Tom and I*)."

   *Strategy:* When you are unsure about a compound like *Tom and ?*, drop the noun and *and* (in this case, *Tom and*). The sentence becomes "The policeman called to ~~Tom and~~ me." Then you can easily see that *me*, not *I*, is correct.

3. *Rule:* When a singular and plural subject are joined by *or* or *nor*, the verb agrees with the nearer subject. For example, "He did not know whether the soldiers or the sailor was (not *were*) telling the truth."

   *Strategy:* You might think to yourself that the closer noun (in this case, *sailor*) has a stronger influence on the verb.

4. *Rule:* Participles are verbs ending in *-ing* (present) or *-ed* (past) and acting as adjectives. A participial phrase must be next to the noun it is referring to. Otherwise it is "dangling." For example, "*Walking down the street,* I saw the house," not "Walking down the street, the house came into view." (The latter sounds as through the house is walking down the street.)

   *Strategy:* The tail on the *g* that ends present participles might be thought of as "dangling," to remind you that whenever you use a participle you need to make sure it is referring to the noun it is near.

5. *Rule: Lay* (present tense) means *to place*. The past tense is *laid*. *Lie* (present tense) means *to recline*. The past tense of *lie* is *lay*.

6. *Rule:* A verb agrees in person and number with its subject. For example, "The landing of the supplies and soldiers has (not *have*) not been completed." (The subject is *landing*.)

7. *Rule:* The *passive* voice is used when the doer of the action is unknown or relatively unimportant. For example, "The plane was

struck by lightning." (Emphasizes the plane rather than the lightning.)

8. *Rule:* A subjective complement completes the meaning of a linking verb like *is*. It refers to the subject and is in the subjective form. For example, "It is he (not *him*)."

To test your memory, turn to page 107 at least 30 minutes after *rehearsing* the material from memory.

### Exercise 8-2

Below are listed six rules of punctuation that students frequently have problems with. The first three have been completed as examples. Develop mnemonic strategies for the other three.

1. *Rule:* When a modifying element restricts or narrows a noun, no commas are used. When it simply adds more information about the noun, commas (or dashes or parentheses) are used. For example:

   The woman, wearing a white dress, will lead the choir. (The woman will lead the choir. By the way, she'll be wearing a white dress.)

   The woman wearing a white dress will lead the choir. (That woman who is wearing a white dress will lead the choir. Not another woman.)

   *Strategy:* In the first sentence, commas are serving as a weak form of parentheses. By thinking of the commas in that way, you should be able to remember that they are used in the nonrestrictive form of the sentence. Like parentheses, the commas mean *by the way*.

2. *Rule:* A semicolon often serves to separate contrasts, as in the sentence "She came to stay; however, she lasted only a week." A colon has the opposite role. It serves as an arrow, signaling that what follows is directly related to the previous statement. For example, "Three factors affect real estate values: location, location, and location."

   *Strategy:* A semicolon is like a red traffic light and a colon is like a green light. You might use a visual association to remember these symbols. In a traffic signal, the red light is on top, just as the dot of a semicolon is on top. A green light is on the bottom, as is one of the dots in a colon.

3. *Rule:* The dash and parenthesis are both used to insert parenthetical comments into a sentence. But while parentheses tone down a comment, dashes emphasize it.

   *Strategy:* You could think of the dashes which "broadcast" a message in Morse code. On the other hand, parentheses look like a fence or clamp that encloses the message.

4. *Rule:* Periods and commas go inside quotation marks. Colons and semicolons go outside quotation marks. For example:

   The article is entitled "How to Do It"; however, it really tells "How Not to Do It."

5. *Rule:* Hyphenate two or more words serving together as an adjective when they precede the noun modified. For example:

   His stories are hard to believe.
   He told one of his hard-to-believe stories.

6. *Rule:* When referring to titles of books or magazines, use italics. For example, *Gone with the Wind* and *Newsweek*, not "Gone with the Wind" and "Newsweek." When referring to titles of articles in a magazine, use quotation marks. For instance, "Life in the Suburbs," not *Life in the Suburbs*.

To test your recall, turn to page 107 at least 30 minutes after *rehearsing* the information from memory.

## REMEMBERING THE FOREIGN LANGUAGES

**Remembering Words.** Ideally, when studying a foreign language, you should reach the point where you can think directly in that language. For example, when you see a door, you think *la porte*, instead of having to translate from English into French.

Nevertheless, when you are first learning a foreign word, a mnemonic aid can be helpful as a bridge between the foreign word and its English equivalent. Once you have filed the new word in your memory and worked with it awhile, the need for the mnemonic bridge disappears.

The Indo-European and Romance languages have many words that sound similar to English words. In many cases, the meanings are also similar. For instance, in German *der Junge* sounds like *young* and means *the boy*.

The relationship between other pairs is a little less obvious. For example, *die Feder* in German means *the pen* and comes from the time when feathers were used as pens.

When these similarities exist, natural associations (see page 16) can be used. But in other cases, the foreign word and its English equivalent have no easily recognizable connection. Then, artificial associations (see page 16), using symbols, can be made.

For example, *Boden* is the German word for *floor. Boden* sounds somewhat like *boat in*. You could visualize a *boat in* the middle of the *floor*.

Many languages have genders for their nouns. For example, German nouns are either masculine, feminine, or neuter, and French and Spanish nouns are either feminine or masculine. To remember the gender of a noun, you could include in your mental image a man or woman to represent the masculine or feminine gender. For the neuter gender you could choose a standard "neuter" object, such as a broom or a lamp, that is always included in the image.

*Boden*, mentioned earlier, is masculine. In your image for *Boden*, you could have a *man* sitting in the boat.

### Exercise 8-3

Develop a mnemonic strategy for remembering each of the foreign words below, its definition, and (for nouns) its gender. The first five have been completed as examples, and a sample mnemonigram is provided for the first one. (Method: pages 26–27.) *Note:* G = German, F = French, S = Spanish, m. = masculine, f. = feminine, and n. = neuter.

1. (G) *das Bilt* (n.) (dahs bilt) — the picture.

   *Mental image:* Someone building (*Bilt*) a picture. Also include a broom (or whatever standard "neuter" object you choose) to indicate the neuter gender.

2. (S) *la caja* (f.) (lah KAH-hah) — the box.

*Mental image:* The word sounds like the "caw-caw" sound of a crow. You could visualize a woman (feminine gender) carrying a *box* with a *crow* in it.

3. (F) *le vedette* (m.) (luh vuh-DEHT) — the star actor.

*Mental image:* Vedette sounds like *the debt*. Visualize a male (masculine gender) *star actor* paying off *the debt*.

4. (G) *der Diener* (m.) (dehr DEE-ner) — the servant.

*Mental image:* Visualize a male (masculine gender) servant serving *dinner* (sounds like *Diener*).

5. (S) *romper* (rohm-PEHR) — to break.

*Mental image:* Visualize children *breaking* toys in a *romper* room (playroom).

6. (F) *mauvais* (mow-VAY) — bad.
7. (G) *steigen* (STEY-g'n) — to climb.
8. (S) *la iglesia* (f.) (lah ee-GLEHS-yah) — the church.
9. (F) *court* (koor) — short.
10. (G) *gelb* (gelp) — yellow.
11. (S) *la mano* (f.) (lah MAH-noh) — the hand.
12. (F) *s'asseoir* (sa-SWAR) — to sit down.
13. (G) *schmecken* (SHMEK'n) — to taste.
14. (S) *la pizarra* (f.) (lah pee-SAH-rah) — the blackboard.
15. (F) *l'oeuf* (m.) (leuf) — the egg. ·

To test your recall, turn to page 109 at least 30 minutes after *rehearsing* these items from memory.

**Remembering Foreign Grammar and Punctuation.** The method for remembering foreign grammar and punctuation is the same as that used for English grammar and punctuation. Refer to pages 72–76.

# 9

# REMEMBERING LITERATURE

Literature is the study of imaginative and creative writing, including novels, short stories, essays, and plays.

Some common memory tasks in literature are:

- Remembering the names of writers and details about them, such as titles of works, writing characteristics, and dominant themes
- Remembering plots, themes, techniques, etc., in literary works
- Remembering names of characters in literary works and details about them

### Exercise 9-1

Develop a mnemonic strategy for remembering each author and the works written by him or her. (Method: pages 24–25.)

1. *James*. The Awkward Age, The Wings of the Dove, The Golden Bowl
2. *Conrad*. Lord Jim, Nostromo, Heart of Darkness
3. *Joyce*. Ulysses, Dubliners, Finnegans Wake
4. *Woolf*. The Voyage Out, Jacob's Room, To the Lighthouse
5. *Faulkner*. Sanctuary, Requiem for a Nun, Light in August

To test your memory, turn to page 109 at least 30 minutes after *rehearsing* the material from memory.

### Exercise 9-2

Develop a mnemonic strategy for remembering each of the following characters from Shakespeare's *King Lear* and the details about each. (Method: pages 23 – 25.)

1. *King Lear.* King of Britain. Tends to be stubborn.
2. *Goneril and Regan.* Lear's vicious daughters, who plot against him.
3. *Cordelia.* Lear's loving daughter.
4. *Edgar.* The Earl of Gloucester's loving, legitimate son.
5. *Edmund.* The Earl of Gloucester's deceiving, bastard son.
6. *Kent.* A faithful courtier of Lear's, who is banished for his straightforward words.
7. *Oswald.* Goneril's steward, who follows the orders of his evil mistress.
8. *Albany,* Goneril's gentle husband.
9. *Cornwall.* The evil husband of Regan.

To test your recall, turn to page 109 at least 30 minutes after *rehearsing* the material from memory.

### *Exercise 9-3*

Develop a mnemonic strategy for remembering, in correct order, the sequence of some major events in *King Lear.* (Method: pages 32–42.)

1. Wishing to retire, King Lear decides to divide his lands among his daughters according to how strongly they express their love for him. When Cordelia, the youngest daughter, states her love in simple terms, Lear becomes angry and disinherits her.

2. Lear also banishes the loyal Kent, who returns in disguise to protect Lear.

3. Lear's elder daughters begin to treat him with increasing disrespect.

4. When Lear realizes his elder daughters want to humiliate him, he goes out into the stormy weather with only his fool as a companion.

5. While finding shelter in a farmhouse, Lear holds a mock trial of his elder daughters. Gloucester brings word that they are plotting to kill Lear.

6. Based on Edmund's evidence that Gloucester is helping Cordelia try to invade Britain, the elder sisters blind Gloucester. Cornwall is mortally stabbed.

7. Edgar finds his blinded father, Gloucester, and saves him from a suicide attempt. Similarly, Cordelia finds Lear, now gone mad, and cares for him.

8. Lear and Cordelia are captured by Edmund after a French army, brought by Cordelia, is defeated. Edmund sends them to prison and issues a secret order for their execution.

9. Goneril poisons Regan in a lovers' struggle over Edmund and stabs herself when her adultery is discovered.

10. Edgar mortally wounds Edmund.

11. The dying Edmund tries to stop his execution order but is too late, for Cordelia is hanged, and Lear dies from grief.

To test your recall, turn to page 109 at least 30 minutes after *rehearsing* the material from memory.

### *Exercise 9-4*

Develop a mnemonic strategy for remembering the techniques that Shakespeare used in *King Lear* to intensify Lear's tragedy. (Method: pages 32–42.)

1. Having Cordelia as well as Lear die.
2. Having Lear go mad.
3. Using the parallel subplot involving Gloucester and his sons.
4. Having Lear banish the faithful Kent.
5. Creating the loyal fool, who reflects on the tragedy of Lear.

To test your memory, turn to page 109 at least 30 minutes after *rehearsing* the material from memory.

# 10

# REMEMBERING MATERIAL
# FOR STANDARDIZED TESTS

The techniques discussed in the preceding chapters can help you prepare for standardized tests like the ACT, SAT, and GRE. For example, as you study the *Cliffs Test Preparation Guide* for the test you will be taking, develop mnemonic strategies for remembering information. A recommended sequence is:

- Determine that you need to remember a piece of information.
- Develop a mnemonic strategy for remembering that information.
- Write your strategies in the margins of your *Cliffs Test Preparation Guide* or on separate paper.
- Rehearse the strategies until you can recall the information from memory.
- Then, take the practice tests provided in your *Cliffs Test Preparation Guide*.

## TAKING VERBAL-ABILITY TESTS

Most standardized tests include a section intended to measure verbal ability. One common type of verbal-ability test contains one or more passages similar to those found in textbooks. Each passage is followed by several multiple-choice questions on the passage contents.

Unlike most other sections of a standardized test, the type of verbal-ability test just described gives you all the information you need to answer the questions. The test is measuring your ability to comprehend written material and, in some cases, make inferences from it. Therefore, in these kinds of tests memory plays a less important role.

However, mnemonic strategies, if used wisely, can help you. The following sequence is recommended for taking a verbal-ability test:

- Skim the question *stems* (not the answer choices that follow each stem) to find out what questions are being asked about the passage.
- Read the passage. First, read just the opening sentence of each paragraph; then read the entire passage.
- Answer the questions, referring to the passage as needed.

As you read the passage, you need to make your mnemonic associations quickly so that you are not spending too much time on them. These associations are intended to help you retain the key information long enough to answer the test questions. Below is a passage similar to those used in verbal-ability tests. The sample mnemonic associations are given in italic type in parentheses.

A phobia is an anxiety disorder characterized by a continuing, intense, specific fear that has no factual basis. (*In a phobia, the "foe" isn't real*.) The person suffering from the phobia may even be aware that the fear is irrational, yet be unable to control it. (*Like most psychological disorders*.) All of us sometimes have irrational fears; it is the intensity of the fear that distinguishes a phobia from less severe cases of fright. (*Visualize someone being very afraid*.) For example, many of us would feel uncomfortable looking over a high cliff edge, but a person with acrophobia (fear of high places) may even refuse to go near a window in a tall building. (*Acrophobia: heights, as in "acrobats."*)

Other common phobias are claustrophobia (fear of closed places), agoraphobia (fear of open places), hematophobia (fear of blood) (*like "hemoglobin"*), ocholophobia (fear of crowds), and monophobia (fear of being alone). (*Mono means "one," like "monorail."*)

Two major causes of phobias are conditioning that leads to avoidance, and anxiety displacement. A person may become conditioned to fear a particular thing and avoid it because of that fear. For example, a child who must walk every day past a house that has a vicious dog may become conditioned to fear dogs in general, and thus avoid them. (*This makes sense*.)

Anxiety displacement occurs when people develop phobias to protect themselves from potentially uncomfortable situations. For instance, if an anxiety-prone woman is being pressured by her family to enter nursing but does not want to, she may develop hematophobia (fear of blood) to avoid the uncomfortable situation. (*This makes sense.*)

Phobias tend to persist because the individual is reinforced by the anxiety reduction that the phobia brings. (*Like how I feel better when not in big crowds.*) One successful form of treatment, called desensitization. (*You are made less "sensitive" to a phobia.*) involves gradual, systematic exposure to the phobic experience until the fear is overcome.

Notice that a variety of mnemonic techniques are used, including:

- Artificial associations (*Phobia sounds like "foe."*)
- Natural associations (*Like most psychological disorders.*)
- Logical associations (*This makes sense.*)
- Visualizations (*Visualize someone being very afraid.*)

However, all the associations are simple and direct. For example, no association was made for the definition of the word *agoraphobia* because none came immediately to mind. DO NOT SPEND A LOT OF TIME WHEN DEVISING MNEMONIC STRATEGIES. USE ONLY THOSE YOU THINK OF AS YOU READ THE PASSAGE.

### *Exercise 10-1*

Below is a passage similar to those found on verbal-ability tests. The parts for which you should try to develop mnemonic strategies are in italic type. Try to use simple, easy-to-develop devices.

Malaria is one of the most widespread diseases in the world. People catch malaria *when bitten by a mosquito that has the parasite Plasmodium* in its salivary glands. The parasite is transmitted into the blood in the form of sporozoites, which first enter the liver cells. *During the incubation period in the liver, antimalarial drugs usually are not effective.*

While in the liver, *the sporozoites go through a process of multiple division, called schizogony, and become merozoites, which enter the red corpuscles.* Once in the red blood cells, the merozoites become trophozoites and evenutally develop into schizonts with black pigment granules. *By schizogony (multiple divison) each schizont divides into numerous merozoites that leave the host cell and enter other red cells.*

When the number of parasites becomes large enough, *usually seven to eighteen days after the person has been bitten, the chills and fever begin.* The interval between fever and chill attacks varies depending on the type of malaria.

*Some forms of malaria may remain dormant for years, possibly due to a small number of parasites in the blood.* However, relapses of the symptoms can occur periodically.

To test your recall of the italic material, turn IMMEDIATELY to page 111.

# Appendix 1
# Practice Tests and Answers

Following are tests to help you see how well you remember exercise material in this book. Fill-in and short-answer tests are used because they challenge your memory to the fullest.

The following process is recommended:

- Follow the instructions at the end of the exercise on which you are testing yourself. Especially, make sure the suggested minimum time has elapsed since you last studied the material.
- Write your test answers in the book or on separate paper. Complete *all* test items.
- Then, turn the page to reveal the correct answers, and score your responses.
- *Very important!* Ask yourself why you got an item correct (what did you do right?) or incorrect (what did you do wrong?). Learn from your successes and your mistakes.
- If you miss more items than you think you should on a test, turn to the page indicated in parentheses. If necessary, change your mnemonic strategies. Take the test again after at least a few hours' delay.

***Exercise 1-1 (5).*** For each name, write the person's occupation. 1. Flagg 2. Cushing 3. King 4. Brooke 5. Barnes 6. Coulter 7. Tarbell 8. Nye 9. Godel 10. Robeson 11. Woolton 12. Limon

***Exercise 3-2 (19).*** Supply the correct objects linked to each word given here. 1. Hive 2. Gun 3. Door 4. Sticks 5. Shoe 6. Tree

***Exercise 3-3 (21).*** List, in any order, the Freudian parts of the human mind and details on each part.

***Exercise 3-4 (24).***
(A.) For each name, write the person's contribution. 1. Dalton 2. Hutton 3. Botticelli 4. Moliere 5. Hertz 6. Hersey 7. Longfellow
(B.) Write the name that corresponds to each of the following contributions. 1. Discovered radium 2. Sculpted *The Thinker* 3. Designed London's St. Paul's Cathedral 4. Painted the *Laughing Cavalier* 5. Wrote *The Cherry Orchard* 6. Described sun-centered planetary system 7. Wrote *The Owl and the Pussy-Cat* 8. Stated the principle of conservation of energy

***Exercise 3-5 (26).*** Give the definition of each word or term. 1. Aorta 2. Palliate 3. Moraine 4. Probity 5. Mummery 6. Torpor 7. Hirsute 8. Igneous 9. Fulsome 10. Gibbous 11. Septum 12. Captious

***Exercise 3-6 (28).*** Pronunciations are given here for the 12 commonly misspelled words in the exercise. Write the correct spelling for each word. 1. pur-son-EL 2. dis-uh-POINT 3. GUY-dunce 4. GRAM-er 5. uh-KWIRE 6. mee-dee-EE-vul (or) med-EE-vul 7. uh-KOM-uh-date 8. full-FILL 9. kon-shee-EN-shus 10. TEM-pruh-munt 11. pree-SEED 12. suh-PRESS

90

***Exercise 1-1 Answers.*** 1. Painter  2. Lawyer  3. Vice-President
4. General  5. Educator  6. Botonist  7. Author  8. Humorist
9. Mathematician  10. Actor  11. Businessman  12. Dancer

Score:___8___Correct

***Exercise 3-2 Answers.*** 1. Apple  2. Orange  3. Baseball
4. Yellow rubber ball with red stripe  5. Lemon
6. Yellow tennis ball

Score:_____Correct

***Exercise 3-3 Answers.*** 1. Id: instinctual, operates on the pleasure
principle.  2. Ego: tries to figure out ways to fulfill the selfish needs
of the id.  3. Superego: opposes the desires of the id.

Score:_____Correct

***Exercise 3-4 Answers.***
(A.) 1. Conceived modern notion of atoms  2. Studied earth move-
ments  3. Painted *Birth of Venus*  4. Wrote *The Miser*  5. Demon-
strated existence of radio waves  6. Wrote *A Bell for Adano*
7. Wrote *Paul Revere's Ride*
(B.) 1. Curie  2. Rodin  3. Wren  4. Hals  5. Chekhov
6. Copernicus  7. Lear  8. Mayer

Score:_____Correct

***Exercise 3-5 Answers.*** 1. Main artery leaving the heart  2. To re-
duce the pain or intensity of  3. Ridge of rocks and mud deposited
by a glacier  4. Reliability (of a person)  5. Ridiculous ceremonies
6. Sluggishness, dullness  7. Hairy, shaggy  8. Rock formed when
molten material solidifies  9. Offensive, based on insincerity
10. Phase of the moon more than half full  11. Wall separating two
cavities  12. Tricky, deceiving

Score:_____Correct

***Exercise 3-6 Answers.*** 1. personnel  2. disappoint  3. guidance
4. grammar  5. acquire  6. medieval  7. accommodate
8. fulfil or fulfill  9. conscientious  10. temperament
11. precede  12. suppress

Score:_____Correct

*Exercise 3-7 (30).* Write the correct date for each event. 1. The Goths invade Rome  2. Start of the Hundred Years' War  3. The Eastern and Western churches split  4. Start of the Spanish Civil War  5. Luther starts the Reformation  6. The French Revolution begins  7. King John accepts the Magna Carta  8. Copernicus claims the sun is the center of our system  9. Napoleon loses at Waterloo  10. Raleigh fails to establish a New-World colony  11. Henry VIII establishes the Church of England  12. The Knights Templar are founded

*Exercise 3-8 (34).* List in any order the names for the four types of igneous rocks.

*Exercise 3-9 (36).* Starting with *kingdom,* list in correct sequence the classification levels used to classify plants and animals.

*Exercise 3-11 (38).* Beginning with the planet closest to the sun, list in correct sequence all the planets of our solar system.

*Exercise 3-12 (39).* List in any sequence the four basic universals of economics present in all economic organizations.

*Exercise 3-13 (40).* List in order of decreasing percentages the eight elements that crystal rocks are composed of.

*Exercise 3-14 (41).* List in any order the five elements that make up the earth's atmosphere.

*Exercise 3-15 (42).* Write formulas for: 1. The relationship among weight, mass, and acceleration due to gravity  2. The area of a triangle  3. The reaction of hydrogen sulfide and sulfuric acid  4. The area of a trapezoid

92

*Exercise 3-7 Answers.* 1. 410  2. 1338  3. 1054  4. 1936
5. 1517  6. 1789  7. 1215  8. 1543  9. 1815  10. 1584
11. 1534  12. 1119

Score:_____Correct

*Exercise 3-8 Answers.* 1. Gabbro  2. Granite  3. Basalt
4. Rhyolite

Score:_____Correct

*Exercise 3-9 Answers.* 1. Kingdom  2. Phylum  3. Class
4. Order  5. Family  6. Genus  7. Species

Score:_____Correct

*Exercise 3-11 Answers.* 1. Mercury  2. Venus  3. Earth
4. Mars  5. Jupiter  6. Saturn  7. Uranus  8. Neptune
9. Pluto

Score:_____Correct

*Exercise 3-12 Answers.* 1. Dividing up scarce resources  2. Distributing goods and services  3. Providing economic stability and security  4. Providing continued economic growth

Score:_____Correct

*Exercise 3-13 Answers.* Oxygen, silicon, aluminum, sodium, calcium, iron, magnesium, and potassium

Score:_____Correct

*Exercise 3-14 Answers.* Nitrogen, oxygen, argon, carbon dioxide, and water vapor

Score:_____Correct

*Exercise 3-15 Answers.* 1. $w = mg$  2. $\frac{1}{2}bh$
3. $3H_2SO_4 + H_2S \longrightarrow 4SO_2 + 4H_2O$  4. $\frac{1}{2}h(b_1 + b_2)$

Score:_____Correct

*Exercise 3-16 (44).* List the following events in correct chronological sequence, and write the details about each.   1. Rise of political parties   2. Louisiana Purchase   3. Hamilton's financial plan   4. War of 1812

*Exercise 3-17 (46).* Complete each of the following statements. 1. The earth's seasons occur because...   2. When adding two square roots...   3. An exterior angle of a triangle is equal to...   4. The indefinite pronoun *each*...

*Exercise 4-1 (49).*
(A.) Write the definition of each term.   1. Endogamy 2. Folk society   3. Ethnocentrism   4. Diffusion
(B.) Write the term which matches each of the following definitions.   1. A class or social group whose membership is determined by birth and whose boundaries are rigidly set   2. The process whereby one group's culture and behavior are adopted by another group   3. One woman married to several men at a time   4. A condition in which members of a group or society have a weakened respect for some of the norms

*Exercise 4-2 (50).*
(A.) For each name, write the person's contribution.   1. Meltzer 2. Money   3. Sorokin
(B.) Write the name that corresponds to each of the following contributions.   1. Conceived the idea of the "looking-glass self" 2. Introduced the concept of anomie   3. Developed a "subcultural theory" to explain urban behavior

*Exercise 4-3 (50).* List the five characteristics that distinguish an industrial society from a youth counterculture.

94

*Exercise 3-16 Answers.* 1. Hamilton's financial plan: Government paid debts; government encouraged economic expansion; government authorized coins and paper money   2. Rise of political parties: Hamilton's Federalist party — strong central government, manufacturing interests; Jefferson's Antifederalists — limited federal government, farming interests   3. Louisiana Purchase: Greatest land deal   4. War of 1812: Causes included violations of U.S. neutrality and U.S. sailors forced into British navy

Score:_____Correct

*Exercise 3-17 Answers.* 1. the earth's axis is tilted   2. combine the numbers under the radical before computing   3. the sum of the opposite interior angles   4. takes a singular verb

Score:_____Correct

*Exercise 4-1 Answers.*
(A.) 1. Marriage within a certain group   2. An underdeveloped, isolated society that is small, intimate, and very cohesive   3. The belief that the behavior and culture of one's own group are superior to those of others   4. The spread of traits from one culture to another
(B.) 1. Caste   2. Acculturation   3. Polyandry   4. Anomie

Score:_____Correct

*Exercise 4-2 Answers.*
(A.) 1. Concerned about the effects of isolation on prisoners   2. Studied sex roles and stereotyping   3. Suggested that societies have "sensate" and "ideational" cycles
(B.) 1. Cooley   2. Durkheim   3. Fischer

Score:_____Correct

*Exercise 4-3 Answers.* 1. Hard work   2. Control over nature   3. Rational approach   4. Future oriented   5. Self-reliance and individualism

Score:_____Correct

*Exercise 4-4 (51).* List the six major ways that people are influenced.

*Exercise 4-5 (51).* List the four kinds of groupings distinguished by Blumer and the details of each.

*Exercise 4-6 (52).*
(A.) Write the details about each of the following historical figures.
1. Randolph   2. Hill   3. Tilden   4. Bingham
(B.) Write the names that match the following descriptions.
1. Montana senator who opposed the Lend-Lease plan   2. American general who surrendered without a fight during the War of 1812
3. First woman candidate for President   4. Secretary of state who purchased Alaska from Russia

*Exercise 4-7 (53).* Write the dates for each of the following events.
1. Japan seizes Manchuria.   2. The Pacific railroad is completed.
3. Aaron Burr kills Hamilton.   4. The Erie Canal is opened.
5. American women gain the right to vote.   6. Congress discusses repeal of the Silver Act.   7. The Panama Canal is finished.   8. President Garfield is shot.

*Exercise 4-8 (53).* List Jefferson's three primary goals for writing the Declaration of Independence.

*Exercise 4-4 Answers.* 1. Information   2. Coercion (force)
3. Referent (modeling desired behavior)   4. Expertise   5. Reward
6. Legitimacy (you ought to do it)

Score:_____Correct

*Exercise 4-5 Answers.* 1. Acting crowd: a temporary grouping with an aggressive goal   2. Expressive crowd: A temporary grouping without a single goal   3. Mass: A large number of people reacting to a common stimulus, such as a gold rush, but acting individually   4. Public: A vaguely defined group of people who, for a time, discuss and disagree about a particular issue—there is no feeling of common identity

Score:_____Correct

*Exercise 4-6 Answers.*
(A.) 1. Virginia Congressman who strongly opposed war with England (War of 1812)   2. American railroad tycoon who hoped to build a worldwide American railroad chain   3. Presidential candidate who won the election but was defeated in the Electoral College by corrupt methods   4. Congressman and painter of political pictures
(B.) 1. Wheeler   2. Hull   3. Woodhull   4. Seward

Score:_____Correct

*Exercise 4-7 Answers.* 1. 1931   2. 1869   3. 1804   4. 1825
5. 1920   6. 1893   7. 1921   8. 1881

Score:_____Correct

*Exercise 4-8 Answers.* 1. To present a theory of government   2. To prove America's determination to be free   3. To use as a propaganda weapon

Score:_____Correct

*Exercise 4-9 (53).* Beginning with Edward II, list in correct sequence six English kings and details about each.

*Exercise 4-10 (54).* List in-correct order the ten Civil War events given in Exercise 4-10 and details about each.

*Exercise 4-11 (55).*

(A.) List the works created by the following artists.

1. Graves 2. Picasso 3. Rouault 4. Marini

(B.) List the artists who created: 1. "The Broken Tree"

2. "The Three Horses" 3. "Bird in Space"

*Exercise 4-12 (56).* Write definitions for the following terms.

1. Minaret 2. Icon 3. Chiaroscuro 4. Pendentive 5. Diptych

*Exercise 4-9 Answers.* 1. Edward II: Weak; barons revolted; his queen had him imprisoned and murdered   2. Edward III: Needed money to fight the French; House of Commons began to control finances; economic crisis, partly due to the plague   3. Richard II: Harshly suppressed a peasant revolt; was defeated by the Duke of Gloucester   4. Henry IV: Had to deal with many rebellions; Parliament gained more financial power   5. Henry V: Won great victories in France, but neglected England; died young   6. Henry VI: Mentally unstable as he grew up

Score:_____Correct

*Exercise 4-10 Answers.* 1. Fort Sumter: Union fort, under Anderson, falls to Beauregard; war is declared   2. First Battle of Bull Run: Generals Johnson and Jackson defeat the Union, under McDowell   3. Shenandoah Valley: Jackson wins many victories, preventing the Union's McClellan from getting reinforcements   4. Seven Days' Battle: Lee forces McClellan to retreat   5. Second Battle of Bull Run: Union badly defeated while led by Pope   6. Battle of Antietam: McClellan forces Lee to retreat after a very bloody battle, but fails to pursue him   7. Emancipation Proclamation: Lincoln announces intention to free slaves in Confederate States   8. Fredericksburg: Burnside makes six unsuccessful charges against Lee's forces   9. Chancellorsville: The Union's Hooker is badly defeated, but Jackson is killed and the South suffers a heavy toll   10. Gettysburg: Lee gambles on invading the North and loses to Meade

Score:_____Correct

*Exercise 4-11 Answers.*
(A.) 1. "Wounded Gull"   2. "The Blue Boy"
3. "The Old Clown"   4. "Horse and Rider"
(B.) 1. Weber   2. Marc   3. Brancusi

Score:_____Correct

*Exercise 4-12 Answers.* 1. Slender tower attached to a mosque   2. A picture of a sacred Christian personage   3. Use of light and dark in a painting   4. Triangular section of vaulting used to support a dome   5. Picture or series of pictures on two hinged tablets

Score:_____Correct

*Exercise 4-13 (56).* List in any order four characteristics of impressionist artists and the names of three representative painters. List in any order three characteristics of expressionist artists and the names of three representative painters.

*Exercise 4-14 (57).*
(A.) Write the definitions for: 1. Syndrome  2. Displacement  3. Heuristics  4. Aphasia
(B.) Write the terms that match the following definitions. 1. Excessive, chronic overeating caused by a brain lesion  2. Visual receptors that give the sensation of color  3. A learned attachment formed during a particular period in an organism's life  4. When a person is told one thing while at the same time receiving opposite signals

*Exercise 4-15 (58).*
(A.) For each name, write the person's contribution. 1. Weber  2. Premack  3. Rosch  4. Galton
(B.) Write the name that corresponds to each of the following contributions. 1. Performed a classic study on problem solving  2. Has studied cultural factors in achievement motivation  3. Found that some instinctive behaviors help survival  4. Nineteenth-century psychophysiologist who studied vision

*Exercise 4-16 (58).* List in correct sequence from lower to higher the stages of Maslow's hierarchy and the details of each stage.

*Exercise 4-17 (59).* List in correct sequence Piaget's stages of childhood development and the details of each. Include the ages by which each stage is usually reached.

*Exercise 4-13 Answers.*

(A.) Impressionists: Technique very important; very colorful; tiny dots sometimes used; concerned about effects of light—Pissarro; Monet; Renoir

(B.) Expressionists: Did not imitate nature; usually dynamic; sometimes abstract—Cezanne; van Gogh; Gauguin

Score:_____Correct

*Exercise 4-14 Answers.*

(A.) 1. A pattern of symptoms that tend to go together   2. The act of using a more available outlet when an impulse is blocked   3. In computer problem solving, a procedure which has often worked before and probably will work again   4. A language disorder caused by a lesion in the brain

(B.) 1. Hyperphagia   2. Cones   3. Imprinting   4. Double bind

Score:_____Correct

*Exercise 4-15 Answers.*

(A.) 1. Developed a formula for measuring differences in sensory intensity   2. Has worked with chimpanzees to study language acquisition   3. Developed the *prototype* theory of meaning   4. Pioneer in the study of individual differences

(B.) 1. Duncker   2. McClelland   3. Tinbergen   4. Hering

Score:_____Correct

*Exercise 4-16 Answers.* 1. Physiological needs: Comfort, sense of well being   2. Safety needs: Security, comfort   3. Love needs: Warm feelings, free expression of emotions   4. Esteem needs: Confidence, self-respect   5. Self-actualization needs: Work, creative, positive thinking

Score:_____Correct

*Exercise 4-17.* Because of the large amount of information involved, the answers to the test items for Exercise 4-17 are not given here. To check your answers, turn to page 59.

Score:_____Correct

*Exercise 5-1 (60).* Complete and balance each of the following equations.   1. $NH_3 + Cl_2 \longrightarrow$   2. $H_2S + O_2 \longrightarrow$
3. $N_2O_4 + H_2O \longrightarrow$   4. $SO_2Cl_2 + H_2O \longrightarrow$

*Exercise 5-2 (61).*
(A.) Write the symbols for the following elements.   1. Tin
2. Iron   3. Lead   4. Gold   5. Sodium
(B.) Write the elements for the following symbols.   1. W   2. K
3. Cu   4. Hg   5. Ag

*Exercise 5-3 (62).* List the mass and charge for alpha, beta, and gamma rays.

*Exercise 5-4 (62).* Write the Atomic Mass Units for:   1. Iron
2. Carbon   3. Helium   4. Aluminum   5. Oxygen   6. Hydrogen

*Exercise 5-5 (63).* Write the electron dot formulas for:
1. Beryllium   2. Oxygen   3. Boron   4. Aluminum   5. Lithium
6. Chlorine   7. Argon   8. Magnesium   9. Phosphorus
10. Calcium

*Exercise 5-6 (64).*
(A.) Write the definitions for the following terms.   1. Mass
2. Acceleration   3. Energy   4. Photon
(B.) Write the terms which correspond to the following definitions.
1. That which is produced by the mechanical disturbance of a gas, liquid, or solid   2. The energy possessed by an unstable object at rest
3. The energy possessed by a moving object   4. The measure of the movement of molecules

*Exercise 5-7 (64).* Write the formulas for:   1. Length contraction
2. Volume of a fluid passing through a pipe   3. Determining the velocity of a bullet

***Exercise 5-1 Answers.*** 1. $2NH_3 + 3Cl_2 \rightarrow N_2 + 6HCl$
2. $2H_2S + 3O_2 \rightarrow 2H_2O + 2SO_2$
3. $3N_2O_4 + 2H_2O \rightarrow 4HNO_3 + 2NO$
4. $SO_2Cl_2 + 2H_2O \rightarrow H_2SO_4 + 2HCl$

Score:_____Correct

***Exercise 5-2 Answers.***
(A.) 1. Sn  2. Fe  3. Pb  4. Au  5. Na
(B.) 1. Tungsten  2. Potassium  3. Copper  4. Mercury
5. Silver

Score:_____Correct

***Exercise 5-3 Answers.*** 1. Alpha rays: mass $= 4$, charge $= 2^+$
2. Beta rays: mass $= 1/1837$, charge $= 1^-$
3. Gamma rays: mass $= 0$, charge $= 0$

Score:_____Correct

***Exercise 5-4 Answers.*** 1. 56 a.m.u.  2. 12 a.m.u.  3. 4 a.m.u.
4. 27 a.m.u.  5. 16 a.m.u.  6. 1 a.m.u.

Score:_____Correct

***Exercise 5-5 Answers.*** 1. 2  2. 6  3. 3  4. 3  5. 1  6. 7
7. Noble gas  8. 2  9. 5  10. 2

Score:_____Correct

***Exercise 5-6 Answers.***
(A.) 1. The quantity of matter, the measure of inertia  2. The rate
of change of velocity with time  3. The ability to perform work
and/or to move objects  4. A particle of light energy
(B.) 1. Sound  2. Potential energy  3. Kinetic energy
4. Temperature

Score:_____Correct

***Exercise 5-7 Answers.***

1.
$$L = \sqrt{1 - V^2/C^2L'}$$

2.
$$V = A_1A_2\sqrt{\frac{2(p_1 - p_2)}{p(A_1^2 - A_2^2)}}$$

3.
$$V = \sqrt{2gh}\,(m_1 + m_2)/m_1$$

Score:_____Correct

*Exercise 5-8 (65).* Write the conversions for the following.
1. One radian = _____degrees
2. One astronomical unit = _____meters.
3. One pound = _____grams.    4. Degrees Kelvin = _____ + °C

*Exercise 5-9 (65).* List in any order four reasons why a person's weight changes as he or she moves across the earth's surface.

*Exercise 6-1 (66).*
　(A.) Write definitions for the following terms.    1. Axon
2. Oogenesis    3. Dendrite    4. Symbiosis
　(B.) Write the terms which correspond to the following definitions.
1. A colorless fluid in the body surrounding many cells    2. A class of vertebrates without jaws    3. The part of a flower that produces pollen
4. The petals of a flower

*Exercise 6-2 (67).* Write the contributions made by the following biologists.    1. Linnaeus    2. Lamarck    3. Leeuwenhoek
4. Harvey    5. Watson

*Exercise 6-3 (67).* List in correct order the stages of cell division and the details of each.

104

*Exercise 5-8 Answers.* 1. 57.3   2. 1.496 × 10$^{11}$   3. 453.6 grams
4. 273.1 + °C

Score:_____Correct


*Exercise 5-9 Answers.* 1. Higher altitude causes less weight be-cause person is further from the earth's center   2. Less weight at the equator because earth's bulge increases the person's distance from the earth's center   3. Less weight at the equator because of centrifugal force   4. More weight where the subsurface rocks are unusually heavy

Score:_____Correct

*Exercise 6-1 Answers.*
(A.) 1. The nerve fiber that conducts an impulse away from the body of a nerve cell   2. The maturation of egg cells   3. The branching nerve fiber that conducts impulses toward the body of a nerve cell 4. The close, mutually beneficial living association of two organisms of different species
(B.) 1. Lymph   2. Agnaths   3. Anther   4. Corolla

Score:_____Correct

*Exercise 6-2 Answers.* 1. Developed a system for classifying organ-isms   2. Proposed that an organism's acquired characteristics could be inherited   3. Pioneered the use of the microscope   4. Discovered the circulation of blood   5. Solved the structure of DNA

Score:_____Correct

*Exercise 6-3 Answers.* 1. Prophase: Chromosomes thicken and the centrosome divides   2. Metaphase: The nuclear membrane disappears and a spindle develops between the two parts of the centrosome — the chromosomes gather on the spindle   3. Anaphase: The spindle di-vides, splitting each chromosome apart   4. Telophase: The nuclear membranes form, resulting in two new cells

Score:_____Correct

*Exercise 6-4 (68).* List in correct sequence eleven of the most important animal phyla and at least one representative animal from each phylum.

*Exercise 7-1 (69).* Write the formulas for the following.  1. The general polynomial of degree $n$  2. The distance and angle for two vectors of the space $V$  3. The derivative when the function for the quotient rule is $f(x)/g(x)$

*Exercise 7-2 (70).* Write the name for each of the following Greek letters.  1. $\sigma$  2. $\nu$  3. $\theta$  4. $\psi$  5. $\rho$  6. $\lambda$  7. $\phi$  8. $\mu$

*Exercise 7-3 (71).*
   (A.) Write the definitions for the following terms.  1. Mode
2. Hypotenuse  3. Median  4. Mean
   (B.) Write the terms that correspond to the following definitions.
1. The horizontal axis in a coordinate system  2. The distance across a circle between any two points  3. The vertical axis in a coordinate system  4. A triangle having two equal sides

*Exercise 7-4 (71).* Write the equivalents for the following fractions.
1. 1/6  2. 3/8  3. 5/6  4. 7/8  5. 5/8  6. 1/8

*Exercise 6-4 Answers.* 1. Porifera (sponges)   2. Coelenterata (corals)   3. Platyhelminthes (flatworms)   4. Nematoda (hook-worms)   5. Annelida (earthworms)   6. Bryozoa (colonial ocean animals)   7. Brachiopoda (lampshells)   8. Echinodermata (starfish)   9. Mollusca (snails, octopus)   10. Arthropoda (crabs, ants, spiders)   11. Chordata (sharks, cod, frogs, snakes, birds, mammals)

Score:_____Correct

*Exercise 7-1 Answers.*

1. $f(x) = f_n x^n + f_{n-1} x^{n-1} + \ldots$   2. (a) $d = \sqrt{(x_1 - x_2)^2 + (y_1 - y_2)^2}$

$+ f_1 x + f_0$ $(n \geq 0, f \neq 0 \ldots$   (b) $\cos \theta = \dfrac{x_1 x_2 + y_1 y_2}{\sqrt{x_1^2 + y_1^2} \; \sqrt{x_2^2 + y_2^2}}$

3. $\dfrac{g(x)f'(x) - f(x)g'(x)}{\{g(x)\}^2}$ if $g(x) \neq 0$

Score:_____Correct

*Exercise 7-2 Answers.* 1. sigma   2. nu   3. theta   4. psi   5. rho   6. lambda   7. phi   8. mu

Score:_____Correct

*Exercise 7-3 Answers.*

(A.) 1. The most frequently occurring score or measure in a group   2. The side of a right triangle opposite the right angle   3. The middle score or number when a group of numbers is arranged in order by size   4. The average, the sum of a group of numbers divided by the number of cases

(B.) 1. X-axis   2. Chord   3. Y-axis   4. Isosceles

Score:_____Correct

*Exercise 7-4 Answers.* 1. .16⅔   2. .375   3. .83⅓   4. .875   5. .625   6. .125

Score:_____Correct

*Exercise 7-5 (72).* Complete each of the following statements of a rule or procedure.   1. A line parallel to one side of a triangle...  2. To solve a quadratic equation...   3. If two chords intersect within a circle...

*Exercise 8-1 (73).* Write the grammatical rule governing each of the following sentences.   1. Seeing my old friend (I cried/tears fell).  2. It is (I/me).   3. Neither the senators nor the president (was/were) willing to discuss the matter.   4. I am the one (who/whom) you will be working with.   5. She addressed the letter to Mary and (I/me).  6. The new building was destroyed by fire (instead of "Fire destroyed the new building").   7. After working he will (lie/lay) on the bed.  8. The wrapping of the parcels (take/takes) about three hours.

*Exercise 8-2 (75).* Write the rule of punctuation that governs each of the following sentences.   1. He was rich (;/:) yet he was not happy.  2. He wrote a magazine article entitled, "Ten Ways to Mess up Your Life (."/".) 3. It was a (well told/well-told) story.   4. The man (who is my father/, who is my father,) will present the award.   5. He read Melville's ("Moby Dick"/*Moby Dick*) for class.   6. His story— and what a story it was—delighted the crowd. (or) His story (and what a story it was) delighted the crowd.

*Exercise 7-5 Answers.* 1. and cutting the other two sides divides these sides into proportional segments   2. (a.) move all terms to one side of the equal sign, leaving zero on the other side (b.) factor (c.) set each factor equal to zero (d.) solve each of these equations (e.) check by inserting your answer in the original equation   3. the product of the segments of one chord is equal to the product of the segments of the other

Score:_____Correct

*Exercise 8-1 Answers.* 1. (I cried) A participial phrase must be next to the noun it is referring to.   2. (I) A subjective complement completes the meaning of a linking verb like *is*. Referring to the subject, it is in the subjective form.   3. (was) When a singular and plural subject are joined by *or* or *nor,* the verb agrees with the nearer subject.   4. (whom) Use a subjective pronoun for the subject of a noun clause and an objective pronoun for the object of a noun clause.   5. (me) A pronoun being used as an object must be objective in form.   6. The passive voice is used when the doer of the action is unknown or relatively unimportant.   7. (lie) *Lay* (present tense) means *to place. Lie* (present tense) means *to recline*. The past tense of *lie* is *lay*.   8. (takes) A verb agrees in person and number with its subject.

Score:_____Correct

*Exercise 8-2 Answers.* 1. (;) A semicolon often serves to separate contrasts, while a colon often serves as an arrow to signal that what follows is directly related to the previous statement.   2. (.") Periods and commas go inside quotation marks; colons and semicolons go outside.   3. (well-told) Hyphenate two or more words serving together as an adjective.   4. (either, depending on intended meaning) When a modifying element restricts or narrows a noun, no commas are used. When it simply adds more information about the noun, commas are used.   5. (*Moby Dick*) When referring to titles of books or magazines, use italics. When referring to titles of articles in a magazine, use quotation marks.   6. (either) Use dashes for more emphasis and parentheses for less.

Score:_____Correct

*Exercise 8-3 (77).* Write the English equivalent for each of the following foreign words. For nouns, include the gender.

(A.) German:  1. steigen  2. (the) Bilt  3. schmecken
4. (the) Diener  5. gelb

(B.) Spanish:  1. (the) caja  2. (the) iglesia  3. romper
4. (the) pizarra  5. (the) mano

(C.) French:  1. s'asseoir  2. l'oeuf  3. (the) vedette
4. mauvais  5. court

*Exercise 9-1 (79).* Write the three works given in Exercise 9-1 for each of these authors.  1. Woolf  2. Conrad  3. Joyce
4. Faulkner  5. James

*Exercise 9-2 (79).* Write a brief description of each of the following characters from *King Lear*.  1. Edmund  2. Goneril  3. Albany
4. King Lear  5. Cordelia  6. Oswald  7. Regan  8. Edgar
9. Kent  10. Cornwall

*Exercise 9-3 (80).* List in correct sequence the eleven major events from *King Lear* given in Exercise 9-3.

*Exercise 9-4 (81).* List in any order the five techniques used by Shakespeare to intensify Lear's tragedy.

### Exercise 8-3 Answers.

(A.) 1. to climb   2. the picture (neut.)   3. to taste
4. the servant (masc.)   5. yellow
(B.) 1. the box (fem.)   2. the church (fem.)   3. to break
4. the blackboard (fem.)   5. the hand (fem.)
(C.) 1. to sit down   2. the egg (masc.)   3. the star actor (masc.)
4. bad   5. short

Score:_____Correct

### Exercise 9-1 Answers.

1. *Voyage Out, Jacob's Room, To the Lighthouse*   2. *Lord Jim, Nostromo, Heart of Darkness*   3. *Ulysses, Dubliners, Finnegans Wake*   4. *Sanctuary, Requiem for a Nun, Light in August*   5. *The Awkward Age, The Wings of the Dove, The Golden Bowl*

Score:_____Correct

### Exercise 9-2 Answers.

1. The Earl of Gloucester's deceiving, bastard son   2. One of Lear's vicious daughters   3. Goneril's gentle husband   4. King of Britain, who tends to be stubborn   5. Lear's loving daughter   6. Goneril's steward, who follows her orders   7. Lear's other vicious daughter   8. The Earl of Gloucester's loving, legitimate son   9. Lear's faithful courtier, who is banished for his frank remarks   10. Regan's evil husband

Score:_____Correct

### Exercise 9-3.

Because of the large amount of information involved, the answers to the test item for Exercise 9-3 are not given here. To check your answers, turn to page 80.

Score:_____Correct

### Exercise 9-4 Answers.

1. Having Cordelia as well as Lear die   2. Having Lear go mad   3. Using the parallel subplot involving Gloucester and his sons   4. Having Lear banish the faithful Kent   5. Creating the loyal fool, who reflects on the tragedy of Lear

Score:_____Correct

*Exercise 10-1 (84).* Answer the following questions based on the passage. 1. Define *schizogony*. 2. What is one possible reason why some forms of malaria remain dormant for years? 3. People catch malaria when bitten by a mosquito that transmits the parasite ___(name)___. 4. During the disease's incubation period in the liver, antimalarial drugs usually ( ) are ( ) are not effective. 5. Through multiple division, sporozoites become ___(name)___s. 6. What usually happens between seven and eighteen days after the person is bitten?

*Exercise 10-1 Answers.* 1. Multiple division   2. A small number of parasites in the blood   3. Plasmodium   4. Are not effective 5. Merozoites   6. The chills and fever begin

Score:_____Correct

# Appendix 2
# Cross Reference to Areas
# of Study

The most commonly offered school subjects are dealt with in Part Two. Below is a list of other topics. If you are interested in one of them, study the pages indicated (in parentheses), which cover the subject or subjects with similar memory tasks.

| SUBJECT OF INTEREST | SUBJECTS WITH SIMILAR MEMORY TASKS |
|---|---|
| Anatomy | Biology (66) |
| | Chemistry (60) |
| Anthropology | Biology (66) |
| Astronomy | Biology (66) |
| | Chemistry (60) |
| | Physics (63) |
| Botany | Biology (66) |
| Computer Science | Math (69) |
| | Physics (63) |
| Drama | Literature (79) |
| Geology | Biology (66) |
| Music history | Art history (55) |
| Philosophy | Psychology (57) |
| | Sociology (49) |
| Statistics | Math (69) |
| Theology | History (51) |
| | Sociology (49) |
| Zoology | Biology (66) |

# CLIFFS NOTES

Ideally, a study guide is like a map through a strange land. If traveling to a strange or new country, one should never go without maps or guides to show what to see, do, and how to react. Likewise, Cliffs Notes offer the readers a guide to the new experiences of each work of literature.

For twenty-five years, Cliffs Notes have helped the student gain increased understanding of literature.

Cliffs Notes provide a good, solid, basic interpretation of the literary work under discussion. They are written by experts — people long familiar with the works.

Cliffs Notes, as well as providing aids to students enrolled in literature courses, present a creative approach to enjoyment of the classics for the adult who finally has the leisure time and interest to investigate the great literature of the world.

Ultimately, reading a Cliffs Note increases and deepens one's appreciation of the literary work and gives greater satisfaction to the act of reading in itself.

For information on the more than 200 titles covering major novels, plays, and poems available in Cliffs Notes, contact your local bookseller or Cliffs Notes, Inc., P.O. Box 80728, Lincoln, Nebraska 68501.

# Cliffs
# Test Preparation
# Guides

Over the years, the art of test-taking has gained
nationwide emphasis. With this in mind, Cliffs Notes has
developed this outstanding series, utilizing the expertise
of Editor Jerry Bobrow, Ph.D., a leading authority in the
field of test preparation. Cliffs Test Preparation Guides
help students achieve the best possible scores on many
of the standardized tests.

With strategies and techniques for answering
questions, and examples of the questions for practice,
the student gains understanding of the test. This
understanding allows the student to relax and do
his/her best.

Cliffs Test Preparation Guides are designed to be
used by the individual. They also can be a valuable tool
for teachers in the classroom setting. Teacher's Manuals
are available for use with Cliffs SAT and Cliffs ACT.

Thirty-minute films (or video cassettes), "Be
Prepared for the SAT (and PSAT)" and "Be Prepared for
the ACT" are available from Churchill Films, 662 North
Robertson Blvd., Los Angeles, CA 90069. The materials
for the films were also developed by Dr. Bobrow.

All Cliffs Test Preparation Guides carry complete
information for the particular qualification test in a
format that does not overwhelm the student. For
information on the fourteen titles in the Series, contact
your local bookseller or Cliffs Notes, Inc., P.O. Box 80728,
Lincoln, NE 68501.